A Complete Guide to Ski Touring and Ski Mountaineering

Including useful information for off piste skiers and snowboarders

HENRY BRANIGAN AND KEITH JENNS

Bloomington, IN  Milton Keynes, UK

AuthorHouse™
1663 Liberty Drive, Suite 200
Bloomington, IN 47403
www.authorhouse.com
Phone: 1-800-839-8640

AuthorHouse™ *UK Ltd.*
500 Avebury Boulevard
Central Milton Keynes, MK9 2BE
www.authorhouse.co.uk
Phone: 08001974150

© 2006 Henry Branigan and Keith Jenns. All rights reserved.

No part of this book may be reproduced, stored in a retrieval system, or transmitted by any means without the written permission of the author.

First published by AuthorHouse   11/30/2006

ISBN: 978-1-4259-7024-6 (e)
ISBN: 978-1-4259-7023-9 (sc)

Printed in the United States of America
Bloomington, Indiana

This book is printed on acid-free paper.

Table of Contents

Inspiration	viii
Foreword	x
About the Authors	xi
Introduction	xii
What is Ski Touring?	xv
1 Uphill Techniques	**1**
1.1 Using skins	1
1.2 Using Harscheisen	3
1.3 Changing direction	5
1.4 Long traverses	10
1.5 Short undulations	11
2 Moving Without Skis	**13**
2.1 Carrying the skis	15
2.2 Moving without crampons	18
2.3 Moving with crampons	24
2.4 Easy summits and ridges	28
3 Tactics Uphill	**33**
3.1 Setting a track	34
3.2 Setting the speed	38
3.3 Moving with the group	40
3.4 Breaks, rest places and ski depots	42
3.5 Movement in avalanche danger areas	44
3.6 Movement over glacier	45

4 Downhill Techniques — 50
- 4.1 Ski techniques – the six basics — 51
- 4.2 Skiing powder — 55
- 4.3 Skiing steep terrain — 57
- 4.4 Skiing in hard and icy snow conditions — 59
- 4.5 Skiing Firn — 61
- 4.6 Skiing crust — 62
- 4.7 Skiing in other situations — 63

5 Tactics Downhill — 66
- 5.1 Choice of route — 66
- 5.2 Skiing with a group — 71
- 5.3 Skiing in avalanche danger areas — 78
- 5.4 Skiing in glaciated areas — 79

6 Safety Techniques — 83
- 6.1 The Rope — 83
- 6.2 Knots — 84
- 6.3 Tying into the harness for climbing — 89
- 6.4 Belays in Snow, Ice and Easy Rock — 89
- 6.5 Use of Belay Devices — 95
- 6.6 Climbing calls — 96
- 6.7 Safety on Glaciers — 97

7 Clothing and Equipment for Ski-Touring — 101
- 7.1 Fabrics — 101
- 7.2 Technical equipment for ski touring — 103
- 7.3 Minimum equipment required to ski tour — 108

8 Practical Avalanche Information — 114
- 8.1 Avalanche types — 115
- 8.2 Snow — 116
- 8.3 Factors that influences avalanche formation — 119
- 8.4 Snow pack examinations — 129
- 8.5 How to make your decision — 134
- 8.6 Tactics on the ground — 138
- 8.7 Search methods — 148

9 A Knowledge of Dangers — 156
9.1 Subjective dangers — 156
9.2 Objective dangers — 159

10 The Weather — 167
10.1 Basic knowledge — 168
10.2 Vertical climate structure — 170
10.2.2 Cloud formation — 170
10.3 Observation of the wind — 174
10.4 Further weather observation — 178

11 Some Rescue and Emergency Techniques — 181
11.1 Crevasse rescue — 181
11.2 First aid and accident procedure — 187
11.3 Snow shelters — 188

12 Planning A Tour — 194

13 Some Navigation Skills — 199
13.1 Understanding the basic winter problems — 199
13.2 Maps and Guide Books — 200
13.3 Other aids to navigation — 207
13.4 Using the map and compass — 211
13.5 Measuring distance — 217

14 Protecting the Environment — 220

15 Some Useful Addresses and Literature — 225

16 Alpine Huts — 227

Inspiration

You set out with the moon still high in the sky, the temperature is cold, the only sound is the comforting swoosh of the skis sliding forward on a cold crisp snow and, the steady rhythmical breathing action of cool fresh mountain air in its most natural form. You can see for miles as the moon lights up the glistening snow crystals ahead of you. The wind whispers to you to move on. You Ski over a landscape unspoiled, the same unspoiled landscape that your descendants might have experienced thousands of years ago.

You ski in one direction, forward, for several hours before deciding to take a rest. You then look round to realise that as far as the eye can see there is no sign of human life or of there ever having been any. The wind has covered your tracks and it is as if you have been transported there by some sort of magic, and you gasp in amazement and realise that life is not measured by the amount of times you breathe but by the amount of times your breath is taken away. And tomorrow, with luck and a new snowfall, you might even experience the same again.

An experience is something which everyone has, and throughout life everyone has an experience, day or an event, which they class as more than special. Everyone who ski tours has at least one ski tour day which they would place in this more than special category. Compared to all the other outdoor adventure sports ski touring has everything. The technical mastery of the skill, the satisfaction of feeling tired from honest physical exertion, exhilaration and trepidation at the thought of what lies ahead, the purity of the landscape, psychological well being, working in harmony with nature and having control over the elements. In the end it is much more than a sport, it becomes a way of life. You see nature showing its full winter beauty not seen by anyone else, a constantly changing landscape that you alone can see, it may be similar next year, or on the other side of the hill as seen by someone else, but it will never be exactly the same. This is the view of a lifetime that is yours and yours alone. This is a feeling of fulfilment that can never be taken away from you. It is a feeling that with luck you can find again, but never need to replace. You are living for the moment, to capture an instant, from an ever changing landscape which is as young as a new born child and as old as life itself. This is not a story about someone else's adventures, it is about you. You can do it. You can have that experience of a lifetime. What are you waiting for, do it now.

Foreword

Participation in all sport can give pleasure and satisfaction. In some sports in particular, participation can lead to moments of exhilaration, elation and memories to be cherished for life. Ski touring and ski mountaineering is one such sport, a fascinating and sometimes complex combination of skiing skills and mountaineering judgement. Whilst a mountaineer on foot is likely to have more time to make critical decisions on route choice and assessment of the prevailing conditions, a mountaineer on skis is potentially travelling much faster so everything can happen so much more quickly. Mountains are a place of great beauty and sometimes peace and tranquillity but they are also a place where the extremes of nature can demonstrate incredible power. Experience and judgement are essential. To quote from the Scottish Mountaineering Club Ski Guide, "Clearly, once technique, nerve and confidence have been developed, the motivated ski mountaineer has magnificent opportunities for exciting adventure". For anyone venturing into a ski mountaineering shop, the ever-changing array of skis boots and bindings and associated equipment is mind-boggling. What equipment do you really need and what are the limitations of its use? Drawing on their extensive experience, Henry Branigan and Keith Jenns have produced a comprehensive guide which will act as a reference for skiers of all levels of ability and experience. Full of useful tips, this is an essential part of your library - read it and prepare for the next ski tour.

Tim Walker

UIAGM

Principal, Glenmore Lodge, Scotland.

About the Authors

Henry Branigan MBE has more than 23 years of ski touring and mountaineering experience, qualifying as a Mountain Guide with the German Army in 1983. He has been a Trainer for the British Association of Snowsport Instructors (BASI) since 1984. Following qualification, he has been actively employed in instructing mountain activities, and has been ski touring all over the Alps, in North America, Scandinavia and in New Zealand.

Keith Jenns has over 15 years experience of skiing and mountaineering and qualified as a Mountain Guide with the Austrian Army in 2003. He is a current Trainer for the British Association of Snowsport Instructors (BASI) and a member of the Association of Mountain Instructors (AMI). He has been a squad member of the Great Britain Ski Orienteering / Biathlon Team and has extensive ski touring experience in Canada, Scandinavia, South America and the Alps. Keith also runs his own outdoor activities company. www.nordicblowfish.com

Introduction

Activities that are carried out in the Alps are continuously developing as people constantly look for different challenges. Ski touring and ski mountaineering have always been there for, what at one time was the specialist, but with progress being made in the development of equipment, coupled with a more affluent society and a more health conscious public who seek quality free-time away from work, ski touring and ski mountaineering are being rediscovered by the masses.

We are also seeing these activities demonstrated on various forms of footwear. There are what we would call the normal ski tourers, with Alpine touring skis or even more traditional Nordic skis on their feet. The snow boarders have now joined them, pushing the limits on every type of ski tour possible. The Telemarkers are not going to be outdone either, as they prove their prowess with a technique as old as skiing itself but as young and exciting as some of those demonstrating it. For those who do not ski we now see snow shoe groups heading for the summits just as well as everyone else.

When we asked ourselves what it was that we particularly liked about the sport, we were surprised to find that we had some very similar reasons but also some totally different, and asking our friends who tour only increased the selection. It became obvious that ski touring offers something for everyone, and what one person dislikes another thrives on.

Someone once told me that a bad day on the hill is better than a good day in the office and that is something we can all relate to. Ski touring has it all - a variety that you will not find anywhere else or in any other sport. The good snow, the bad snow, the long climbs, the short climbs, the fantastic downhill runs, the not-so-fantastic downhill runs, views that just cannot be captured well enough on camera to describe what you actually saw, the challenges, the satisfaction, the friendships bonded with childish laughter at the bottom of a powder run or after having had a narrow escape from some moment of danger, the combination of physical ability with technical know-how in a slick operating team, and the trust that you put in your partner's ability to rescue you if it is required. You might not notice all of this on your first tour but as time goes on, and you start pushing your own limits, then you will know what we are talking about.

By bringing out this book we hope to give you a knowledge of the skills required to ski tour successfully and safely, but not only that, we also hope that some of our own enthusiasm for the sport will rub off on you and spur you on to ever increasing discoveries about yourself and the environment that you are in.

We have put together a number of chapters that cover the subjects which we feel are important, if not essential, for enjoying ski touring. Some of the topics have specialist books written about them and here we have tried to condense what is important for the person on the ground, without excluding the important points. Although we are professionally employed in the mountains, we are foremost enthusiasts writing about our experiences of ski touring.

We hope our knowledge and experience will be useful for those coming into ski touring for the first time but our intention is also to aid the more experienced tourer and provide guidance on leading groups within the Alpine environment.

It would give us great satisfaction if this book encourages you to go out and try ski touring. It would give us even more pleasure if in the future we were to bump into you somewhere on tour or in a mountain hut.

Henry Branigan and Keith Jenns

What is Ski Touring?

There are various descriptions given to **Ski touring** which can be purist descriptions, but in reality much of the same equipment is used and the activities are locked together under the one overall description of **Ski Touring**.

Ski Touring, itself, is generally described as an activity where someone skis uphill in order to ski back down again without the need to take the skis off. Numerous people for numerous different reasons partake in this form of activity and the ability to ski to a high level is not a necessity. There are the summer walkers who would like to move about in winter, the good skiers looking for an off-piste challenge or powder snow, and those looking for freedom or to escape the every day stresses of life. For some it just provides a different form of exercise or an opportunity to meet new people; the list is almost endless.

A **Ski Mountaineer,** on the other hand, is someone who uses their skis to get to the bottom of a mountain, takes the skis off to climb the mountain and then either skis down or walks back to their skis and skis out again. The reality now is that some of the more advanced tours may require the 'tourer' to leave the skis at a so called 'ski depot' in order to take in easy summits on foot which may or may not require some mountaineering skills. **Ski Touring** and **Ski Mountaineering** therefore combine into the same activity.

Telemark Ski Touring is an activity that is also very popular these days. The main difference here is the equipment and a little bit of technique. The skis and boots are designed to allow the skier to perform the age old turn of Telemark. The Telemark skier is capable of doing all the normal ski techniques and because of the design of boots, bindings and skis, is also able to perform the Telemark technique.

Nordic Ski Touring is normally performed on gentler undulating terrains. Here there are a number of differences. The skis and boots would be similar to Telemark in purpose, but much lighter. Wax may also be used, instead of skins, for grip when the uphills are not so steep; this gives a much faster forward glide. Longer poles are used to help with forward glide and a lighter glove system is used.

There is also the phenomenon of the increasingly popular **Piste Touring**. In fact, up until a couple of years ago it was so limited in popularity that a name had not been created for this 'new' discipline. It is now so much in 'vogue' that it has created, certainly in some places, some problems for lift companies. The 'Piste Tourer' skis up the piste in the evening and waits for the piste machines to prepare the piste, then either skis down late at night, or waits until first light to carve the perfect tracks. Unfortunately, this can damage the freshly pisted slopes, which then freeze over, creating a substandard piste for the paying customers the next day. For the 'tourer' it is a fantastic experience, providing a simpler version of the traditional form, allowing beginners, those with limited time or who have no partner to ski with, a safer and inexpensive form of exercise and exhilaration.

Off Piste Skiing or **Heli Skiing**, are very good for improving your ski technique and, although they use the same safety skills and techniques covered in this book, are not categorised as **Ski Touring**. They both require some form of lift system to get to the top of the mountain, in order to ski back down and, although someone **Ski touring** might use a lift system to assist in going uphill, it is purely being used to get to a point where the individual can commence further uphill skiing.

With all of the variations described above, it is possible to undertake one day tours, ski from hut to hut, ski on glaciated or non-glaciated terrains, or travel over several days at a time. The Alps provide a huge playground to combine such mediums; varied terrains, versatile hut systems, complex weather, and magnificent views all adding further to the variations and complexities of '**Ski Touring**'. Each variation in turn requiring a different understanding of the hazards involved; each one providing a unique experience.

One of the good things of any ski tour is the company that you keep.

1 Uphill Techniques

As in all alpine activities, success in ski touring is based upon taking the opportunities when they are offered. The decision of whether or not to take the opportunities is based upon having an understanding of the risks and the safety elements which are involved, and matching ability to ambition. To move safely and enjoy success in ski touring it is important to master some techniques, allowing as controlled a descent as snow conditions and a heavier rucksack will allow, and in ascent allowing for forward speed with minimum energy output. As well as understanding the techniques required, it is important to know when and where to implement them. This comes with experience - a progressive experience gained from planning correctly and with an honest appraisal of ones ability. To start with we are going to look at the techniques required when moving uphill.

1.1 Using skins

Skins are used on the base of the ski when moving uphill. They allow you to slide forward but grip in the snow to stop you slipping backwards. Moving with skins is similar to a very basic form of Nordic skiing. It is a rhythmic shuffle, shifting the weight from one ski to the other which allows the ski tourer time to look around. An almost automatic action which lets the tourer concentrate on using the track and the lay of the land correctly as well as watching out for any danger. The method of putting skins on varies depending on the type. It is good to have the skin folded in half or even better to have both ends folded into the middle which makes it much easier to work with, especially when windy. Keep the sticky part of the skin out of the snow.

Moving uphill using skins.

Technique points:

- Skis should be normally hip width apart allowing the feet to move freely past one another.

- Make a definite shift of the weight from one ski to the other.

- Try to weight the whole foot as you push off.

- The unweighted ski should be slid forward without lifting it off the snow. (When setting a track in fresh, heavy snow it is required to lift the tip out of the snow before pushing it forward).

- The head should be held up to allow for easier breathing and orientation.

- Length of pace should shorten as the hill steepens. (If you need to use the heel raisers then the length of pace would also get shorter).

- The ski poles are used more on the flat for support and balance and on the steeper slopes to assist the leg action.

- When using the ski poles the arms and hands should be kept low to minimise muscle work and also to avoid the rucksack strap rubbing under the arms. This also lets the blood flow to the fingers more easily, keeping them warm in cold conditions.

- The ski is kept as flat as possible to allow the maximum amount of skin to grip. To achieve this it is often necessary to push the knees away from the hill and not into the hill, as would be normal when skiing downhill.

Top tips:

- As far as snow conditions and terrain allow, you should try to ascend on skis using skins, this being the fastest and most comfortable way of moving.

- When moving across areas where water is visible try to avoid getting the skins wet as this could possibly lead to the skins freezing and icing over.

- When resting on tour avoid warming the skins up too much in the sun as this could also lead to icing over once you start moving again.

- Keep the skins in good condition, carry some spare glue to keep the skins on and skin spray to avoid icing over. A hard wax can also be used to rub over the skin to prevent icing.

- Short steep and icy patches can be crossed using a side step action or herringbone.

- On longer traverses it is useful to use the heel raiser on the downhill ski only, as this makes it more comfortable to move. In addition to this the hand in the uphill ski pole is often taken out of the strap and held lower down on the pole.

1.2 Using Harscheisen

Something which is a nuisance to carry, but should not be left behind, is the harscheisen or ski crampons. When conditions are icy or the snow is very hard, using the harscheisen in conjunction with the skins will make movement much easier. Looking ahead and making your decision early to put them on in easier ground is much safer than waiting until you really need them but find yourself in an awkward position. However, Harscheisen should only be used when necessary as they decrease the forward speed, and the lack of glide tends to rub more on the feet.

Harscheisen should be used in icy conditions or hard packed snow.

Technique points:

- Technique is similar to moving with skins on but the harscheisen do not allow as much glide.

- When sliding the ski forward a slight lifting of the ski is allowed to avoid catching of the harscheisen or tripping on them.

- Length of pace would be shorter than when moving with skins only.

Top tip:

- When using harscheisen, concentrate on placing all points into the snow. Putting the ski on its side edge only increases the likelihood of bending or damaging the harscheisen.

1.3 Changing direction

When moving uphill on skis it is advisable to try to use the lay of the land and take one long easy angled line to the top. This is not always possible and when it is required to change direction you should try to do this without losing the rhythm. The following techniques are used when changing direction uphill.

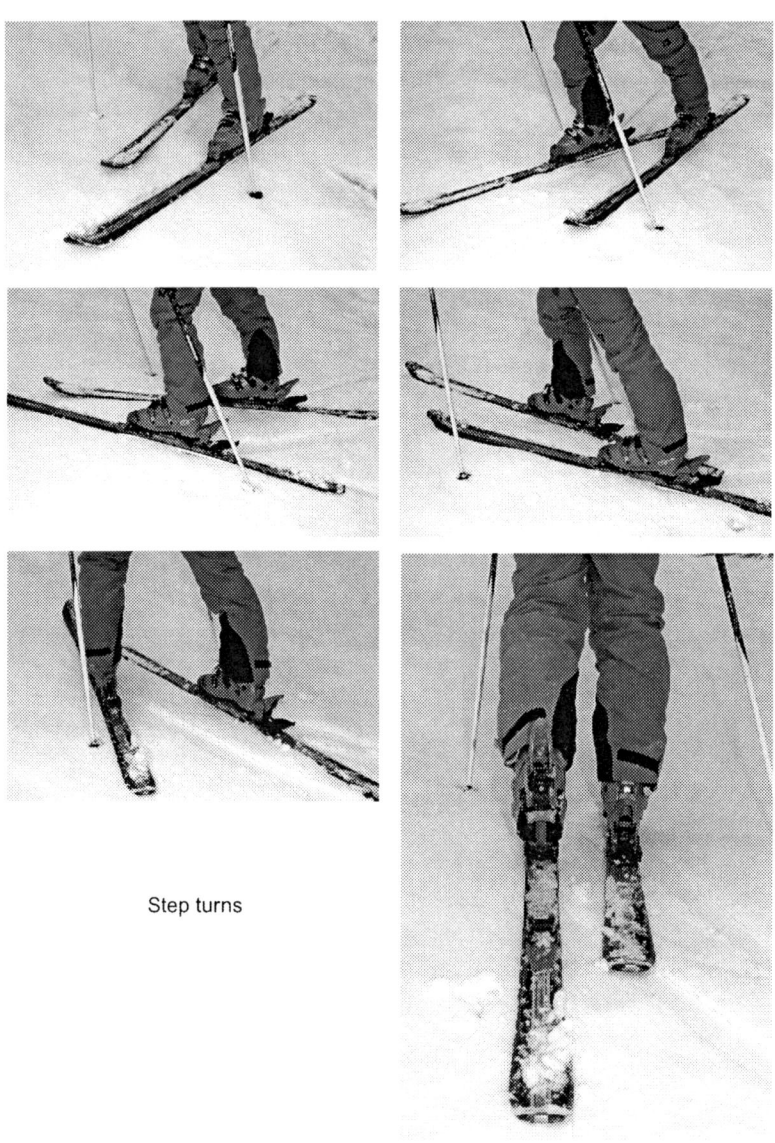

Step turns

A Complete Guide to Ski Touring and Ski Mountaineering

1.3.1 Step turns

Type one step stem. On easier angled slopes the idea is to move the tip of the inside ski into the new direction as a step and to stem the outside ski out, whilst maintaining a normal forward movement. Forward rhythm and pace length should not change.

Type two step. On slightly steeper slopes it may only be the inside ski that is stepped into the new direction and the outside ski closes parallel to this. The aim is still to step round without losing forward rhythm and pace length.

Sharper turns can be gained on steeper ground by changing the pace length and shortening the rhythm of forward movement.

1.3.2 Kick turns uphill

If the slope is too steep for stepping round, then a kick turn is used. When moving uphill, an uphill kick turn is far more favourable than a downhill kick turn. This is one of the most underrated techniques in ski touring. A poor kick turn when you are going uphill for a couple of hours could cause you misery, energy sapping slips, a rise in stress levels, not to mention the danger of falling on icy ground and landing back where you started. Pay attention here and try to master it.

Technique points for type one:

- To start with bring the skis into a horizontal position and, if needs be, stamp in a bit of a platform. This avoids any chance of the skis sliding back downhill.

- The poles initially are placed to the side for support. Downhill pole slightly forward and the uphill pole slightly back.

- The uphill ski is turned into the new direction with a swing action of the leg. The change of direction is about 120°, and the feet should be vertically in line and fairly close together.

- The poles can now be placed uphill for support, and the full weight transferred onto the uphill ski.

- Here comes the trick. The trailing ski (which will be the new uphill ski when you move off) is now brought round into the new direction by rolling the tip of the ski round the leading boot, this avoids any chance of catching the ski on the snow on the uphill side and tripping over.

Kick turn uphill type one.

Technique points for type two:

- This technique is the same until you bring the trailing ski round. Here, instead of rolling the tip around the boot, the ski is lifted a little sideways and the heel of the boot kicked onto the ski bringing the tip up. This allows a much faster turning action than type one.

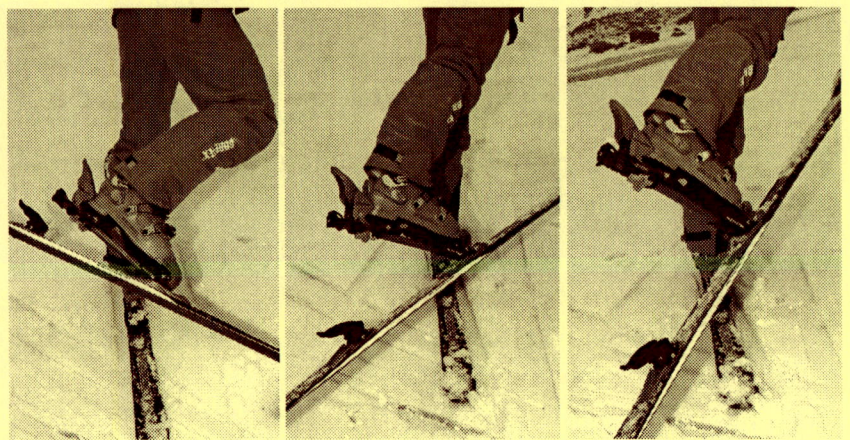

Kick turn uphill type two.

Top tips:

- Try to make the whole action as flowing as possible in conjunction with your forward movement. This avoids holding up anyone who is directly behind you and also helps to keep your own rhythm going.

- When moving up a longer hill using kick turns the group should spread out a little. The idea is to move into the corner as the person in front of you moves out. This allows everyone to keep a steady pace. The leader waits for everyone at the top.

- On no account should you try to catch up with the person in front after a corner. This forces the people further back in the group into a series of interval training sprints.

1.3.3 Kick turn downhill

The downhill kick turn is not favourable when moving uphill. It has the disadvantage that you lose a little height when using it. It also puts you in a very uncomfortable position and in this position there is a greater chance of tripping and falling face first downhill. This type of fall is much more difficult to recover from than one when you are already facing into the hill. However, there are times when it is an advantage, for example in very deep new snow.

Kick turn downhill.

Technique points:

- For a start position, move the skis horizontally across the hill and stamp out a bit of a platform.

- Face downhill and place both poles uphill for support - one either side of the body.

- The lower ski is lifted round into the new direction with a swing of the leg.

- Weight is transferred onto the lower ski.

- The upper ski is now brought round into the new direction along with the ski pole.

Top tip:

- In the middle of this movement both skis are on the ground and facing opposite directions. This is very bad for the knees. To avoid this, begin to move the weight onto the lower ski before it comes into contact with the snow. Now, to avoid falling over, the trailing ski must be brought round quite quickly.

1.4 Long traverses

A long traverse can be quite a weary business due to the fact that one ski is constantly higher than the other. A well laid track should try to minimise this where possible and when it is not possible to avoid then a few technique tips might help to ease the pain.

Technique points:

- When traversing hard packed snow slopes keep the track on as shallow an angle as possible.

- If the slope is icy for short stretches it may also be advisable to take a slightly downhill line to be safer and quicker.

- On longer stretches of icy slope put on your Harscheisen. (Preferably put them on early and in a comfortable position than wait until you are on the ice)

- It is also possible to use the heel raisers on the downhill ski only, to balance the level of the feet.
- The uphill ski pole can be held further down the shaft and the hand of the lower pole placed on top of the pole as this will help a little with the balance.

Top tips:

- In soft snow try to lay the track closer together. This may help to bring both skis to the same height.
- On hard or icy snow, on moderate slopes, try to keep as much of the skin on the snow as possible.

1.5 Short undulations

For short downhill sections within an overall up-section it can often take longer to take the skins off and put back on again than it would do to simply slide down the hill with the skins on.

Sliding downhill with skins on.

Technique points:

- In order to maintain balance the skis are kept at normal hip width with one ski slightly forward than the other. This could look like a very basic Telemark position.

- If the forward ski catches on anything then be prepared to step forward with the trailing ski thus avoiding the obvious dive forward that could be caused by the bindings not being clamped down.

Top tips:

- Changes in direction should be done with stepping or kick turns. Any foot turning movement should be avoided as this may push the skin off the ski.

- On slightly longer downhill stretches it is possible to lock the bindings down giving extra support.

2 Moving Without Skis

Moving without skis on your feet is used when it is technically and physically easier than moving with skis on, or if it is going to be safer because of possible subjective danger. Before taking the skis off, however, ensure that the snow conditions will allow you to go on foot.

There are various criteria to consider before making your decision to go on foot:

- What type of snow surface do you have (soft, hard or icy)?
- How steep is the slope?
- How long is the area that I have to cross?
- If I have to cross rock is it snow covered, loose rock or ice covered?
- If I slip on the way over what will the consequences be?
- What equipment do I have at my disposal?

Top tips:

- If you think you might have to move on foot then make your decision early so that adjustments can be made in a comfortable position.
- Can I move without crampons? Again, decide early as trying to put crampons on after you have already started sliding is not a good idea.
- Can I move without safety rope and equipment?
- Are there any safety precautions that I should implement before I move into the danger area?

Short scrambles are often required to reach the summit.

2.1 Carrying the skis

There are various ways of carrying the skis and the method to use mainly depends on the type of snow and terrain that you are crossing and whether you are ascending or descending.

Carrying the skis on the rucksack

2.1.1 Skis on the shoulder

If the passage to cross is only short and hands are not needed for forward momentum or to climb, then the skis can easily be carried on the shoulder.

Technique points:

- Both skis should be attached together with some form of strap. There are plenty of options for this available in almost any ski shop.

- Both poles are put in the free hand and used for support (normally on the uphill side).

Skis crossways on the rucksack

Skis crossways on the rucksack

On slightly longer passages, and where there are no obstacles on the side, it is possible to attach the skis crossways under the lid of the rucksack. This is particularly useful when going downhill and facing downhill.

Technique points:

- Both skis should be attached together as previously described.

- The skis should be placed under the lid of the rucksack and firmly tied in with the centre of gravity of the skis in the middle.

- The poles can now be used for support, balance or to assist in forward momentum.

2.1.3 Skis vertical on the side of the rucksack

If the passage to cross is narrow and does not allow much room for moving around then it is advisable to have the skis vertical on the rucksack. Examples of areas where this would be used are: walking through villages, climbing passages, woodland and gullies.

Technique points:

- The skis are fixed left and right on the side of the rucksack.
- The ski tips can be joined together with a strap.
- It is better to have the skis as high as possible to avoid catching the calf muscles on the tails or even catching the tails in the snow, causing a possible trip.

Skis vertical on the rucksack for short climbing passages.

2.2 Moving without crampons

2.2.1 Moving in soft snow

Moving uphill with ice axe and ski pole.

If the snow is soft enough that good grip can be gained, and footsteps kicked into the snow, then it is safer to go without crampons. Be aware that an ice layer could be under the soft snow and all grip could be lost.

Technique points going uphill:

- Fast movements, especially when there is a thin crust on soft snow, can sap energy quicker than anything you have done before, therefore move slowly, place your feet positively and shift your weight from one foot to the other to create a firm base before you try to step up on it.

- Keep the length of pace short. Large steps require more energy.
- Tilt the foot into the hill to avoid sliding back out.
- Try to keep the breathing rhythm as relaxed as possible.
- The poles are held fairly low to avoid lifting the arms too high. On steep slopes it might also be good to have both poles together and laid flat in front of you in the snow to assist in pulling yourself uphill.

Top tip:

- The skis should be carried either vertical on the side of the rucksack or crossways under the lid.

Technique points when traversing:

- When traversing slopes it might be useful to have both poles on the uphill side and to lean on them slightly for support.
- On steeper traverse areas it is better to face into the slope and step sideways with the poles held in one of the above methods.

Top tip:

- Skis are best carried vertical on the sides of the rucksack.

Technique points when going downhill:

- Upper body leans slightly downhill to help avoid feet slipping away from you.

- Keep the steps short to avoid sinking in too deep and starting a forward dive downhill.
- Poles are used on both sides for support.
- On steeper slopes it is often better to face into the slope.

Top tip:

- Skis are best carried crossways on the top of the rucksack.

2.2.2 Moving in hard-packed snow

The hardness of the snow, the steepness of the slope and your confidence in your ability are the deciding factors for moving on hard-packed snow.

Technique points moving uphill:

- The feet are kicked strongly into the snow pack. A swing of the leg is used to assist this.
- The foot is angled slightly into the slope to give a better platform.
- Make a definite weight transfer from one foot to the other.
- Keep the length of pace short.
- Ice axe or ski poles or a combination of both can be used depending on your confidence or, rather, your ability.

Top tip:

- Skis are carried either vertical or crossways on the rucksack.

Technique points when moving diagonally uphill or in a traverse:

Cross over step

- Either walk forward in a cross-over step or face inwards and move with a side step depending on your confidence level.

- Use slow, steady, precise movements.

- Small steps are safer.

- Ice axe (if used) should be held in the uphill hand with the pick facing backwards, ready to go into an ice axe arrest position.

Top tip:

- Skis should be carried vertical on the rucksack.

Technique points when moving downhill:

Moving downhill with good heel support.

- Move facing either out/downhill or in/uphill depending on your confidence level. If you are unsure then face in, as it is easier from this position to recover from a slip.

- Feet are kicked into the snow using a strong leg swing.

- If a slide is possible use your ice axe.

- Descending straight down is easier than having to cross the feet when moving down and sideways.

Top tip:

- Skis should be carried crossways on the rucksack.

2.2.3 Actions on taking a fall

Even when your technique is good there are times when you might lose your footing and start sliding downhill. A momentary lapse in concentration; an icy layer not noticed. In such circumstances quick actions are required to stop the slide before any speed is picked up.

Ice axe arrest position without crampons.

Technique points:

- Roll onto your stomach, feet downhill, arms and legs spread wide.

- Use feet and hands to dig into the snow and at the same time lifting the stomach, chest and hips off the snow.

- If using an ice axe it should be used to stop the slide by holding it diagonally across the chest, being careful not to poke yourself in the face or stab yourself in the leg (your face should be turned away from the adze) and the pick dragged in the snow to slow yourself down. With this method chest, stomach and hips are on the snow to put more weight on the axe and the feet, especially if wearing crampons, are off the snow.

2.3 Moving with crampons

Certainly when skiing in glaciated areas, and also sometimes in non glaciated areas, it is possible to have conditions that require the use of crampons. Moving with crampons requires a certain amount of practice to master the techniques. Without some form of proficiency you are likely to find crampons more of a hindrance than a benefit, but with the correct technique you will find that using crampons can allow you to move over icy ground comfortably, quickly and with the minimum of effort. The hardness of the snow/ice and not the steepness of the slope should be the decisive factor on whether to use crampons or not. This chapter restricts itself to the important points for the ski mountaineer and does not go into the specialities of the ice climber.

Hard ice requires the use of crampons.

2.3.1 Flat foot technique

This is the most common technique used in moderately steep ground.

Technique points:

- When walking forward try to place as many points of the crampon in the snow as possible.

- Feet are placed slightly wider apart than normal to avoid tripping over the other foot and the toes are pointed slightly outwards.

- As in all the other techniques so far, energy is saved by moving slowly and precisely and by being very deliberate about placing the feet correctly.

- To avoid the snow balling up under the feet and causing a possible slip it is necessary to hit the crampons with the ice axe every few steps. More modern crampons come with an anti-balling plate.

- An ice axe is normally used, but ski poles can also be used in combination with the axe.

- When moving diagonally uphill a cross-over step is used and the feet pointed slightly downhill to make it easier to get maximum crampon points in the snow.

- The ice axe should be held in the uphill hand.

- When moving downhill the knees are flexed and pushed over the feet with the upper body bent forward.

- Short steps are used.

Top tip:

- If being carried, the skis can either be vertical on the rucksack or crossways on the way up, and crossways if moving downhill.

Snow covered rock

2.3.2 Front pointing

Front pointing showing different axe positions.

On steeper ground this is the most common technique used and is put into practice when it becomes too uncomfortable on the ankle to try anything else.

A Complete Guide to Ski Touring and Ski Mountaineering

Technique points:

- The feet are held in a position where the toes point to the snow, allowing the front points to anchor in the snow.

- The feet are kept slightly further apart, to avoid one crampon catching on the other.

- The feet are kept horizontal, allowing the calf muscles to relax a little and giving better anchor with the front points. Too low with the heels and the front points slip out; too high with the heels and the boot hits the ice first causing the foot to bounce away from the ice before the crampons can grip.

- The body is kept fairly upright.

- One steady swing of the leg should be enough to anchor the front points. Avoid trying to kick holes in the snow.

- The axe can be used as an extra anchor giving more safety when moving the feet.

- Use small steps.

- Technique going straight up and straight down is almost identical, although steps tend to be shorter when going down.

- When moving across the slope, again, the technique is almost the same. Keep the axe in the hand of the direction you are heading in, Use short steps to avoid over stretching, and when closing the trailing foot do not allow it to close too tightly to the other foot - hip width apart is ideal.

Top tips:

- If you are carrying the skis on the way up, the choice is either vertical on the side of the rucksack or crossways on top. If you are going down or across the slope then it is better to have the skis vertical.

- It is possible on not so steep a slope to combine the various techniques to ease the tension on the muscles.

2.4 Easy summits and ridges

It is not always necessary to heave up when a push will do just as well.

There are many ski touring summits that are crowned with a rocky outcrop forcing you to leave the skis behind, go on foot, and do a little scrambling. Mastering the basics of scrambling and moving on rock will make these passages much safer for you, but the overall important factor is to gauge your ability correctly. Remember the complications: stiff boots, icy rock, cold, wind, wet, snow-covered rocks and, last but not least, remember climbing back down is always harder than climbing up.

Using the front of the boots on small foot holds.

Try to maintain a good balanced position.

A Complete Guide to Ski Touring and Ski Mountaineering • 29

Technique points for the basics:

- Always try to stay in balance on the rock.

- Keep the heels lower than the toe on the rock. Lifting the heels high pushes the toes off the rock.

- Keep your hips away from the rock so that you can see your feet.

- Try not to overstretch with the feet or hands as this brings you off balance.

- The rock in the mountains can often be quite loose. Check the rock for stability first, then think about pressing into the rock when you pull up and not away from the rock.

- Check the rock for stability before you put weight on it.

- Try to step up with the legs as opposed to pulling with the arms.

- The hands can be reversed to push up from as well as pull up.

Technique points for climbing down:

- Facing into the rock is normal but it is difficult to see your feet. Technique for this is simply the reverse of climbing up.

- Facing away from the rock - this is more comfortable, and easier to use on chimney type passages.

- Sideways down climbing. This is used on slightly easier passages where the rock-side arm is used for support. A zigzag direction is used, where possible, to swap the weight from one side to the other.

Climbing down facing away from the rock.

Climbing with crampons

On mixed ground, where you have to cross icy slopes and rocky outcrops, it can be too awkward, dangerous or time consuming to continuously take the crampons off and put them back on again. At times like this the problem is moving over the rocks with the crampons on.

Technique points with crampons:

- Keep the feet horizontal.
- Use the front points where possible.

- Use small steps.
- Only climb facing into the slope. This goes for climbing up, across and down.

Using crampons on rock.

3 Tactics Uphill

When planning a ski tour either at home or from the valley base it is important to include some kind of routine for the way up. The more information you have at your fingertips the easier it is to plan (maps, guide books, information from magazines, information from friends who have done the tour).

A well placed track takes the line of least resistance up the hill and avoids as much danger as possible.

When planning the tour you can decide:

- The choice of route
- The rest places
- The equipment you require
- The time necessary

A Complete Guide to Ski Touring and Ski Mountaineering

When planning your routine it is also important to stay flexible, as conditions on the ground may require changes to your original plan.

A ski touring group on route.

3.1 Setting a track

You can tell a lot from looking at a ski track. An uphill track should take the line of least resistance up the hill, avoiding any dangers, rounding the different terrain formations in a smooth, energy-saving steady climb. The track width should be comfortable for others following to ski in. In fact, a well-laid track shows the ski touring skill, or lack of it, of the person who set it. The following are points to consider when setting a track:

When skiing in areas with obvious signs of avalanche danger, it is important to keep some spacing between the group members.

Techniques for general ground observations:

- Take an overall view of the ground every time you come into a new panorama.

- Look at the avalanche situation and make a decision on the dangerous and unfavourable passages.

- Watch out for other alpine dangers.

- Decide where the steep and flat passages are.

- Make a decision on how good the snow surface is. This could be new soft snow, hard icy snow, etc, and note it for the way down.

- Is the ground in front of me (taking into account my observations, my equipment and my ability) safe to cross?

- Where can I lay a track here that is avalanche safe, crevasse safe, fall free and energy saving?

- Where are my escape routes or alternatives?

- Decide whether the conditions on the ground have changed in any way from the plan that you made.

Deciding where to put your track will depend on the result of these observations. If there is already a track available then this should be checked for its safety using the above criteria.

Avalanche situation

The avalanche situation is the absolute governing factor on where to lay a track or whether or not to follow a track already there. Because this is such a complex subject, a chapter is dedicated to it later in the book.

Other alpine hazards and dangers

- A safe distance should be kept from cornice areas and steep ridges.

- Hanging glaciers and ice fall areas should be avoided.

- Bad visibility blocks the ability to make a good observation of the danger ahead.

- In spring time you should avoid areas under rocky outcrops where there is evidence of rock fall i.e. rocks lying on the snow surface.

Top tip:

- Ice avalanches from ice fall areas or hanging glaciers are not dependant on temperatures. They can come down at any time. Low temperatures do not necessarily offer extra safety.

Slope steepness

The steepness of the slope should, where possible, be selected to allow an energy saving, rhythmical progress. The steepness should, where possible, lie between 20-25°. This is obviously dependant on the snow condition and the individual's ability.

Snow conditions

The snow conditions actually decide whether the way up is going to be a fairly easy-going event or a strength sapping affair. The decision between good and bad conditions is often very close and is reflected in the following criteria:

- Aspect of the slope
- Type of slope
- Altitude
- Weather history

Passages with unfavourable snow conditions should be avoided.

Top tips:

- Gullies and bowls are the sort of areas to avoid as these are where snow builds up.
- Steep wind blown slopes are difficult to negotiate.

Ski touring groups laying an undulating track through the landscape.

3.2 Setting the speed

The speed that you move forward in ski touring is very important. Ski touring can put extra strain on the body that you might not encounter in summer activities in the mountains. Strenuous track setting in fresh powder snow, as well as unfavourable weather conditions, can certainly wear you down quickly. When setting off it is important to allow the body time to adjust to the activity. As in any sporting activity that you do, a set warm-up period is required in order to get the muscles and the flow of blood adjusted correctly to the exertion. It is therefore better to set off slowly as this also allows everything to settle properly, socks in the boots, rucksack straps and clothing. Fifteen to twenty minutes should be allowed for this, followed by a short rest to adjust any clothing or equipment. Too fast a pace at the start will only result in blisters and exhaustion. Remember that one person can normally move a lot faster than a group of about six people, so if you are setting the pace for a group go even slower.

Technical points:

- Always have something in reserve in case you have to up the pace in an emergency.

- The length and type of tour should be considered when setting the pace.

- Ideally you should go at a pace that generates enough heat to keep warm but not too much that you are dripping in sweat, which then means that you get cold quickly when you stop.

- A pace that allows a conversation to take place is a good indicator that you have got it right.

- Some snow conditions are faster than others and allow a longer stride. When changing from one snow to another remember that the person at the back requires more time to get into the faster snow.

- Some areas are more technical than others. Again, before racing off, remember that the person at the back may need more time.

- It is comfortable for a group to stay in the same track as the leader and even go stride for stride, allowing everyone to get an even breathing rate.

Top tip:

- The correct clothing is obviously important. Too much and you overheat, too little and you get cold. Keep hats, head bands and gloves in a pocket so that you can put them on when you are on the move and not have to hold up the group every five minutes to get them out of your rucksack.

3.3 Moving with the group

The person taking responsibility for the group should be sorted out right at the beginning, to avoid any arguments later when people are tired. If it is a guided group, it is simple - the guide is at the front, sets the pace and makes all the decisions on responsibility for the group. When no guide is available, the responsibility often falls to the most experienced. If it is debatable as to who might be the most experienced then it is better to debate it in the comfort of the valley and not when the decision is required on the hill.

The size of the group can have a positive, as well as negative, effect on the tour. Groups of between three to six people should be the norm.

If the group is too large

- The leader has a more difficult job on all safety aspects.
- With small technical problems too many people are standing around.
- It is difficult to keep an eye on what everyone is doing.
- Larger groups generally move slower and require more time for the tour, thus leaving less time in reserve.
- The concertina effect is much greater i.e. slow-fast-slow-fast. This is a very energy and morale sapping process for the people further back in the group.
- The amount of success on the tour is normally decreased.

If the group is too small

- It can increase the danger on glaciers of falling in crevasses.
- It puts a lot more strain on individual group members when setting a fresh track.

Top tip:
- It is often an advantage to split down a large group into two smaller groups.
- If you are at the front and move from slow snow into fast snow, spare a thought for the people at the back. Do not speed up until everyone is in the fast snow.

Order within the group

The order within the group should be carefully thought about and the strengths and weaknesses of each member taken into account. The following points should be considered:

- The person accepted as being the leader should go in front. When it is heavy-going it is acceptable to be in second position but still controlling the front.
- Weaker members should be near the front in order to get a better track and a steady pace (but not at the front).
- The strongest member of the group, not the leader, should go at the back.
- The distance between group members should be so that no one steps on the others skis and at the same time no one lets the gap get too big.
- Avoid having a lot of totally inexperienced people in the group. Some may be better skiers, some better mountaineers, but a whole group with neither of these skills is a liability.
- Change the order round to suit the group's skills to the ground ahead.

If you take your skis off to move onto the summit, think about the danger of your skis sliding off down the hill without you.

3.4 Breaks, rest places and ski depots

These should all be planned ahead as they are a key element to the comfort and safety of the group and add to the eventual success of the tour.

Breaks

How often and for how long should be purposely built into the plan. Weather, snow conditions and the physical and technical ability of the group should be taken into account.

- A short break after 15-20 minutes is normal to allow adjustment of clothing.

- At each hour a break for drinks and a snack of about 5 minutes.

- At approximately 2½-3 hours a longer break of about 30 minutes.
- When weather allows, a break on the summit to enjoy the scenery and take in the value of the day.
- At each stop announce how long the break will be as this allows everyone in the group to organise themselves as they see fit.
- At each stop protect from getting cold. Put on a windproof jacket or some warm clothes.
- Use the time to adjust any clothing or sort minor kit problems.
- Use the time to check navigation. There is nothing worse than having to stop five minutes after a break in order for the leader to check navigation, when it could quite easily have been done during the break.
- Do not leave any rubbish behind.

Rest places

A good rest place is not just somewhere where you stand still; it must fulfil some criteria to be classified as good

Keep your rest places in a sheltered and safe area.

- It should offer safety from any danger (avalanche, crevasse, cornice, ice and rock fall).

- It should offer protection from the elements, especially the wind. Stay in the sun when it is cold and in the shade when it is warm.

- It should offer a good view of the panorama to give an inner feeling of wellbeing.

- It should not be in an area that interferes with the nature or wildlife.

- It should not be directly before a hard climb.

Ski depots

Ski depots are usually put in just before a steep summit ridge, when there is not much more to be gained by going on ski and carrying the complete rucksack with you. Ski depots should be decided early, with suitable space for the whole group. The higher you go the less likely you are to find something suitable. A ski depot should have the same criteria as the rest place - certainly as far as safety goes. Anything being left at the depot should be well secured against the wind or possibility of someone knocking the kit over and having it roll downhill. Skins should be removed from the skis, in preparation for the downhill, before heading off for the summit.

3.5 Movement in avalanche danger areas

The correct behaviour in avalanche danger areas reduces the risks considerably. Again, because this is such a complex subject, a chapter is dedicated to it later in the book.

Sometimes the only difference between a safe route and a dangerous route is the snow condition.

3.6 Movement over glacier

Skiing over glaciers is, in some people's opinion, the most exhilarating and exciting aspect of ski mountaineering. The requirement and responsibility of both the leader and the group members is far above that of touring in non-glaciated areas.

It is possible to move without roping up when there is no danger of falling in a crevasse.

The added requirements are:

- A knowledge of glaciers - how the glacier moves, where crevasses form, where the danger areas are.

- The ability to observe and decide how dangerous the crevasses are.

- An understanding of how and when to rope up.

- The ability to do a crevasse rescue.

Choice of route

The main criterion here is safety. The track should be set over ground free from crevasses, or at least where there are not so many crevasses, and away from any other dangers.

Observation of the crevasse danger

How well you observe the crevasse danger depends entirely on how much you understand about the glacier. Without knowing how the glacier is built up, how it moves, where and why crevasses are formed, it is very difficult to move safely over it. Deciding when to rope-up, or even if to rope-up, can be the difference between a safe, comfortable crossing or a disaster.

Temperature, weather conditions, snow conditions, and the lay of the land also play a key-role in your decision.

It is possible to move without a rope when:

- After considering all the elements it is decided that there is no danger from falling in a crevasse.
- When the glacier is covered in a very cold hard snow pack, mostly found early in the morning.
- In a winter with a lot of snow fall.
- When you know the glacier from the summer to be free from crevasses.

Top tips:

- If in doubt, rope up.
- When moving without a rope make sure you still have your harness on.

You must move on the rope in the following circumstances:

- The glacier is unknown to you.

- In ice fall areas or in areas where it is possible to have lots of crevasses.

- After new snowfall, especially when accompanied by wind.

- During bad visibility.

Top tip:

- Make your decision based on your knowledge and experience, not because of what you see other groups doing.

Order within the rope team

The order within the rope team can increase the safety of the group if you use the individual skills well. On the other hand it can increase the danger if you do not consider some of the following points:

- The leader should go at the front using knowledge and experience to avoid any danger areas. Should the risk of the leader falling into a crevasse become so great that it is likely to endanger the rest of the group, the leader would go in second place - thus steering the person in front and also being in a better position to set up a rescue.

- The more experienced and stronger/heavier members of the team should go directly behind the leader. This is the number two on the rope in a three person team. In a four person team the number two and three on the rope would be next in experience to the leader. It is the job of the number two to hold the leader in a fall and also fix an anchor position.

- The distance separating members of a rope team is dependant on the amount of people in the team and the size of the crevasses. More details of this are given in the chapter on rope knowledge.

How to move with the rope

- Try to have the whole team moving at right angles to the crevasse so that only one person at a time is exposed to the risk of falling in.
- If you have to move in the direction along the line of the crevasse then you should not follow the track of the leader but move in your own track so that the team is still at right angles to the crevasse.
- The pace should be a little slower to allow everyone time to keep the rope handling tidy.
- The rope should always be as taut as possible.
- When changing direction, try to keep the same distance apart.
- When resting, on no account close up as this leads to the possibility of everyone falling into the same crevasse.
- Where there is an obvious snow bridge, only cross one at a time.

Top tip:

- Think ahead that there may be a call of nature as no one is allowed to leave the rope team at any time.

4 Downhill Techniques

Skiing downhill is, for a lot of ski tourers, the high point of any ski tour. For some it is the only reason for going touring, although I do know some who dread it because of their lack of technique. In order to enjoy downhill, in any snow condition and in any terrain, it is important to have a variety of techniques up your sleeve and to know when and why to use them. This can also be looked at from a safety prospective. The better a skier can negotiate a downhill run, the less chance there is of having an accident. Whatever your ability, it is important to do what you do well, in order to minimise the risk of falling over and injuring yourself, thereby becoming a liability to your other group members. If all you can do is a traverse and kick turn, then make it a good one. In order to improve your technique, spend some time under instruction. Some instructors from the British Association of Snowsport Instructors are trained off piste and are capable of offering the perfect solution.

A point to note: This is not a ski instruction manual. There are enough of them on the market. This chapter is limited to giving you some tips on techniques and how to implement them in different terrain and snow conditions.

Good powder snow allows enjoyment for every ability

4.1 Ski techniques - the six basics

Every technique you use to ski downhill is affected by what you do with the six basics. Controlling these basics decides how well or how badly you ski. There is some space for error between one end of the movement/position and the other and, as long as you read the snow and terrain well, you should be capable of getting down any slope with an element of control and, at the same time, look fairly good.

Success, "I stayed on my skis".

4.1.1 Ski position

An open parallel stance allows the feet, legs and skis to be moved easier and allows easier turning and edging of the skis, which is more important when using carving skis or heavy waisted skis. This also helps the sideways balance and, with that, overall stability. There is also less chance of crossing the skis over.

A closed parallel stance blocks leg movement, but this more solid block position of the legs is useful in soft powder snow as the legs sink evenly into the snow making control much easier.

With a stem position of the uphill ski it is possible to shorten the length of time that the skis stay in the fall line, therefore making it easier and quicker for you to get around the corner without accelerating. This also allows you to cut down the requirement for vertical movement.

4.1.2 Vertical movement

By using vertical movement of your body to move into and out of the turn it is possible to move smoothly from one turn to the other. This vertical movement aids the ability to turn and edge the skis. To move into the turn the ankle, knee and hip joints are extended and to finish the turn the same joints are flexed. The amount (or range) of movement required depends on the snow, steepness of the slope and speed of forward movement. It is also possible to change the power or speed of the movement to suit different snow conditions. Heavy snow or crust that makes it difficult to turn the skis require an explosive movement to get the skis to move, whereas a smooth more gentle movement on a good firm base allows easy steering of the feet and at the same time is very economic with energy output.

4.1.3 Arm and pole position

The ski pole can be used for a couple of different purposes.

A pole plant used in conjunction with the above mentioned vertical movement aids the stability and balance of the turn and adds to the rhythm of the whole process.

A pole plant used for support in the turn, or to help a push off, is brought into play when a more explosive vertical movement is required (narrow gullies - where a jump turn might be required). Regardless of use, it is important to keep the arm movement to a minimum cutting out any possible shoulder and upper body movement.

4.1.4 Weight shift

In normal cases, when making a turn, the ski on the outside of the turn is weighted more than the ski on the inside of the turn. This is particularly important in hard snow conditions when weight on the inside ski could lead to a fall if the ski is not edged properly. In softer snow the inside ski is also weighted, although not quite 50/50. Too much weight on one ski in soft powder will result in the skis sinking to uneven levels in the snow, normally resulting in a spiral fall. This slight shift in weight from one ski to the other should, in soft powder, be a smooth, flowing transition and not very noticeable to the naked eye. An abrupt shift in weight (as in an uphill stem turn used mainly on hard snow) is a very visible action and normally from an open ski stance. Where should the weight be on the ski? This is a question often put to me. When stretching the legs in vertical movement the pressure is more on the ball of the foot, and towards the end of the turn the pressure comes a little further back from the ball of the foot towards the heel. You are trying to maintain a dynamic balance on the skis. That means the skis are always moving, changing speed, direction and angle. The snow condition may change abruptly causing the skis either to rush forward or to slow down sharply, and as the angle of the slope changes, so do the skis and therefore the body should adjust accordingly.

4.1.5 Steering and edging the skis

In order to achieve an effective turn it is important during the vertical movement (the extending and flexing of the legs) that the legs are turned slightly on their vertical axis and pressed inwards. This allows the feet to turn the skis, and the knees to press inwards thereby tilting the skis onto the edges and giving overall control to steering the skis through the turn. It is important that the legs work independently of the upper body i.e. the upper body is not allowed to turn with the skis. The amount of edging varies, depending on snow conditions, and is very important in icy conditions. When using carving skis the turn can be achieved simply by edging and weighting the skis and allowing the skis to run along the edge. This cuts out any sideways movement of the skis.

4.1.6 Upper body movement

If the legs are steering in the direction of the turn it is important, in order to maintain balance, that the arms and upper body counter this by turning slightly more downhill. This is especially important in narrow gullies where jump turns are used with a lot of leg movement and little time between turns to allow correction of body position. Otherwise, a more neutral upper body position can be held, as in skiing powder, but still minimising any swinging of the upper body. When carving it is certainly possible on piste to allow the upper body to lean into the inside of the turn. However, remember when ski touring you are likely to be carrying a heavy rucksack and to swing the upper body around too much could result in back injuries.

Training on piste before heading off on tour.

4.2 Skiing powder

Powder skiing is the reason a lot of people go ski touring - skiing through powder which is fluffing up around your head, effortlessly sliding through turn after turn. However, this only happens when you have a grasp of the technique required. The basic technique in powder is a variation of the parallel turn, which is characterised by rhythmical turns in a short to medium radius. The difficulty with powder is that if you allow the skis to get completely under the snow, the weight of the snow creates a very laborious task when trying to turn them. Added to this is the need for more forward and sideways balance.

Good powder technique

Technique points:

- The skis are in a closed stance. An open stance allows snow to get between the skis and can push the skis further apart than is comfortable.

- Towards the end of the turn more weight is placed towards the heel of the boot (a sort of bounce) thereby allowing the ski tips to rise to the surface.

- The ski pole on the downhill side is moved into position before the turn comes to an end.

- As the tips come out of the snow you will feel a letting up of the grip of the snow on the skis. At this time you can allow the legs to stretch a little.

- As the legs extend they should also be turning the skis into the new direction with the upper body rotating forward accordingly to stay in balance. Do not allow the legs to extend fully as this is a very unstable position. If needed, extend the legs half-way and then pull the feet up towards you a little to.

- Depending on the radius of turn that you want, you can tilt the skis over more onto the edge. This is not to have the edges gripping in the snow but to allow the base of the ski to push against the snow.

- It is important to try and keep an even rhythm from turn to turn and from one turn going straight into another with a continuous change in ski pressure. Do not allow the skis to go into a traverse.

Top tips:

- For every type of powder and steepness a set forward speed is required in order to allow the skis to ride up out of the snow. Too slow and you use a lot of energy and make life technically difficult for yourself. Too fast and you are liable to lose control.

- The radius of the turns should suit the speed and angle of terrain. Short to medium radius are normal.

- If you have not yet mastered the correct technique but need to get down a hill quickly and safely, then think about using a traverse with a kick turn, or snow plough turns. Alternatively, a very good learning progression is to use garlands (these are half turns where you only turn into the fall line and out of it to the same side every time).

- When moving into a new slope where you are unsure of the snow condition, do a few garlands to get started and to build up some rhythm.

- Powder skiing may look easy but you can expect to be breathing heavily at the bottom of the hill. Also if you have to pick yourself out of the snow a few times with a heavy rucksack on it can be very tiring indeed, not to mention time consuming. If, towards the end of the day, you are already tired at the top of the hill then think about taking the easy option down - traverse kick turn and stay on your feet.

4.3 Skiing steep terrain

Being able to ski on steep terrain safely is an absolute must for most ski tours. It can happen on easier tours that a slight lapse in concentration on route finding brings you onto a steeper slope than you expected to be on. You are then faced with the choice to either ski it or skin back up to get back on route. On the longer hut to hut tours you will normally come across steeper slopes on a daily basis, some as much as 40º. It is not essential to look stylish, but a good, solid, sound technique will allow you to ski steep slopes confidently, and relatively comfortably, with enjoyment. The technique for steep slopes requires a very positive outside ski steering which allows good control of speed and line. A fairly open ski position with a shorter radius is preferred.

Some steep areas require a little assistance.

Technique points:

- Towards the end of a turn there is a very dynamic flexing of ankle, knee and hip joints with the skis turned across the fall line to control the speed.

- To start the next turn the pole on the downhill side is brought forward.

- An explosive extension of the legs assisted with support from the pole plant. This movement should be directed downhill and slightly forward, and not just forward or upwards. The skis are turned quickly over the fall line.

- When weighting the skis, a strong steering action of the outside ski continues to have the skis turning and the upper body tilts forward and downhill over the downhill ski.

- The outside arm prepares early for the next pole plant and, to help avoid rotating too much, the forearm and hand are opened slightly.

Top tips:

- When skiing into a steep slope, start slow and controlled to get a feel of the snow conditions.

- When people ski steep slopes they are not used to, there is an almost automatic longing to lean uphill. This must be avoided at all costs, as it will almost certainly lead to a fall.

- On steep slopes of about 40º the explosive extension of the legs can mean that the skis leave contact with the snow making it easier to turn the skis. This can be built on with an extension of legs then a leg retraction (pulling the feet up towards you gives you more time in the air to turn the skis).

- If you know you are skiing steep slopes and conditions are going to be icy then make sure your edges are sharpened up.

4.4 Skiing in hard and icy snow conditions

Particularly in spring when there has been a lot of melt freeze, and in the early mornings before the sun hits the snow, it can be rock hard. This type of condition requires an aggressive edge to your ski technique. The main emphasis being on the outside ski but also with inside ski edge to help with control. The skis are held in an open position allowing for better leg movement and edge control on both skis. Short aggressive turns are used.

Icy conditions on the glacier.

Technique points:

- Throughout the whole turn try to move the weight from the ball of the foot to the heel and emphasise this open ski position.

- The upper body moves forward and downhill over the outside ski.

- Towards the end of the turn the skis are turned almost across the fall line, edged to the extreme, and weighted to cut the forward speed of the skis almost to a stop. At the same time the pole is planted on the downhill side.

- From this position the skier is almost catapulted forward downhill, allowing the skis to be turned and placed on the new edge.

- Strong flexing of the legs, steering and edging to finish the turn off.

Top tips:

- Good fitting boots, well prepared skis and edges are a big winner here.

- Even the best technique and prepared skis do not always solve the problem on hard ice. Either try to ski around the difficulty or side slip over it, with style.

- To ski ice fast and controlled requires a lot of physical effort and a positive, active attitude. To keep safe and minimise the risk of falling...do not go for it half-hearted.

4.5 Skiing Firn

Next to skiing powder, this is probably the best loved snow condition to ski on. Cruising turns with very little effort or energy output, on a firm base with about one inch of firn (just when the sun begins to melt the snow - sometimes called spring snow). This can be as good as the best piste conditions, characterised by smooth vertical movement and flowing shift of weight, accompanied by a light pole plant action. The ski position is whatever suits the skier. However, if you have left it too late and the sun has been on the slope for longer, then it is much more complicated. You have a base that will not support you and a lot of wet heavy snow making it very difficult to turn the skis. This requires an explosive extension of the legs and early turning of the feet as well as an even weighting of both skis towards the end of the turn. The ski position is a narrow parallel one or closed. Middle to long radius are preferred.

Technique points:

- From the end of one turn, and with support from a pole plant, an explosive stretching of the legs moving the body forward and turning downhill. So much so that the skis are totally unweighted.

- The skis are turned under the body.

- Both skis are evenly weighted towards the end of the turn.

- As the skis come through the fall line, the turning of the upper body is checked to avoid over-rotating.

Top tips:

- Skiing this deep firn snow, and any snow which is heavy and making it difficult to turn the skis, requires a controlled speed. Too slow requires more energy and pressure on the knees and makes it very difficult to turn the skis.

- Skiing in a closed ski position and weighting skis evenly prevents one ski sinking or digging in more than the other one.

- The tips of the ski must come up, even if you lean back a little on the skis, but you must get back in balance again over the skis - at the latest when the skis are beginning to turn over the fall line.

4.6 Skiing crust

Skiing crust is a nightmare for many ski tourers but even with good planning of the tour it is sometimes unavoidable. Whether it has been caused by wind action or melt freeze, it can be skied. Dynamic leg action, skis turning in the air, support from a pole plant and short radius turns are the way ahead.

Sometimes the snow supports you, sometimes you break through

Technique points:

- From the end of the turn, the upper body is clearly leaning forward and downhill.

- Forearm and hand are slightly opened downhill ready for a supportive pole plant.

- After an explosive stretching of the legs the feet are drawn up (retracted) underneath the body, and the skis turned out of contact with the snow.

- As the skis are turned in the air, the body can straighten out slightly and prepare for the next pole plant.

- On landing, the legs are strongly flexed and the upper body rotated forward and downhill.

Top tips:

- A shorter radius turn in crust is fairly strenuous, but leads to much safer skiing than a longer radius.

- Rhythmical controlled turns from one turn to the next and not too slow.

- With a heavy rucksack or when in a physically tired state, it is too difficult to use this technique. Here the answer would be to do long traverses, and even kick turns.

4.7 Skiing in other situations

Here we are looking at the following situations:

- Skiing on a glacier
- Skiing roped up
- Skiing in a track/following in line

- Skiing slopes where there is a danger of dropping off the edge
- Skiing in bad visibility
- Skiing when extremely tired

These sorts of conditions are seldom seen on shorter ski tours, but when ski mountaineering or hut to hut touring you will more than likely be confronted with them. For this reason one technique should be mentioned that will allow you to overcome everything with relative ease - the uphill stem turn. It can be used in almost any snow condition, any type of terrain and also at very slow speed.

Using an uphill stem in light powder.

Technique points:

- At the end of a traverse or turn, the uphill ski is stemmed out unweighted and placed onto its inside edge. At the same time the downhill pole is moved forward in preparation for a pole plant.
- With a pole plant, the lower leg is stretched and the weight shifted from this ski to the stemmed ski.

- The outside leg is now flexed and the ski steered through the fall line. The inside ski can either be steered or stepped in parallel to the other one.

- Upper body leans forward and downhill.

Top tips:

- Depending on conditions you can use this turn in long or short radius, or in conjunction with a traverse.

- You can vary the angle of the stem to suit your speed. Larger stem for slow speed; narrow stem for faster speed.

- When very tired or in bad visibility or simply when it is not very favourable to do much vertical movement with the body, then a wider stem can be used to steer the skis safely through the fall line.

- A slight variation in icy conditions, or for a much smoother turn, is to stem the ski out at the same time as the stretching of the legs and vertical movement of the body.

Enjoy yourself.

5 Tactics Downhill

Along with achieving the aim of the tour, the downhill part is one of the highlights. Planning the downhill section should take into account the maximum safety of the group, combined with the maximum excitement and satisfaction. Whereas the uphill track takes the line of least resistance up the hill, the downhill track is set in the steepest area (that your ability can cope with), the best snow and most fun.

5.1 Choice of route

As in the uphill, the downhill part of a ski tour should be well planned in advance in order to avoid unpleasant surprises. The aspect which offers the best powder or firn snow is normally taken, depending on the avalanche state. However, this tends to be truer with day tours than with tours over several days.

A good line brings added safety and enjoyment. In order to avoid ending up in a dead end, decide in advance where the route goes and keep a constant eye on the overall direction.

When planning the tour you should decide on:

- The area of the ski off
- The route you want to take
- Any rest places you intend to take
- A rough idea of the time it will take you

Top tip:

- In bad conditions (visibility, avalanche danger, lack of local knowledge) you should stay close to the uphill track.

5.1.1 Track choice

A good track shows not only that the leader skis well, but that the leader has also managed to keep a close eye on all the safety aspects whilst still enjoying the descent. Some observations that you should be making are:

When choosing a line, safety must be the first consideration. You can start thinking about it before you get to the top.

- A change in snow conditions may require you to change your technique.

- Watch what the snow is doing. Has it been in the sun? Is it in the sun now? Is it in the shade? Has it only just started to be exposed to the sun? All of these indicate that the snow condition might change.

- As first choice the track should be taken to avoid avalanche danger; as second choice for enjoyment.

- Look out for changes in the ground that might put more stress on the snow to cause an avalanche.

- The speed that you ski down can often put you on the wrong course and into danger areas. Keep an eye on the compass and altimeter.

Negative points often seen on the descents

- The overview of the ground is generally more difficult than on the way up.

- Terrain and conditions change quickly.

- Critical observations are often missed or ignored.

Positive points often seen on the descents

- Making a wide detour to avoid dangers is a lot easier than on the way up.

- Critical slopes can be assessed at the top of the slope and, depending on the danger, a decision made on whether or not to ski down.

5.1.2 Other alpine dangers

As on the way up, an eye should be kept on the possibility of other dangers: a drop off, ice fall, steep slopes covered in ice, rock fall, rocks in the snow causing the skier to fall. Most of these are easy to ski around. If it is not possible to avoid these dangers, it may be essential to slow down and to spread the group out.

Remember, just because someone else has got down does not mean that the slope will not avalanche.

The most suitable angle for the downhill phase is about 30°, but this is also getting into the most suitable angle for avalanches. Watch out!

5.1.3 Snow conditions

It is often said that you cannot select your own snow for the downhill ski, and if you just leave things to chance then this is probably true. By making well thought out observations, however, you can select the best of what is there.

A Complete Guide to Ski Touring and Ski Mountaineering • 69

- The snow pack, altitude, aspect, wind, temperature, time of day, time of season, sun, shade, weather, terrain, and history are all observations that you should be making.

- In early season, good and bad conditions are often fairly close together - mainly due to wind.

- In late season and spring, the aspect of the slope and the time of day are key elements.

- A little bit of sun, even in cold conditions, can put a thin crust on the surface, whilst in the shade powder snow is still to be found.

- In extremely bad weather conditions you can get just about every type of snow on the same ski down. Move a few metres over and try your luck there.

5.1.4 The correct tactics

- The correct tactic goes a long way in preventing accidents.

- If you cannot see over the brow, ski slower and make a new appraisal.

- When entering the top of the slope make a few controlled turns or half turns to get a feel for the snow.

- When skiing down wider ridges, stay away from the corniced side.

- In spring, be aware that the rivers underneath may have started flowing causing some thin snow bridges to form.

Snow conditions and group ability decide what the tactics are going to be.

5.2 Skiing with a group

When you watch some groups skiing downhill you often get the impression that it is just a wild bunch on a charge, throwing all caution to the wind, showing no consideration for safety or for others, and totally oblivious to everything around them. The leader of a group has the responsibility to bring the group safely into the valley but at the same time giving every member of the group the chance to have a personal and satisfying experience - not always an easy job. By sticking to some well-planned guidelines laid out below, this task can be made a lot easier:

- No one skis past the leader unless instructed to. The leader has the experience to read the snow and observe the dangers.

- The person appointed to stay at the back (normally one of the better skiers, complete with some first aid stuff and repair kit), stays at the back and does not overtake anyone - especially someone who has fallen. It is easier for the tail person to ski down to a casualty than it is for the leader to get their skins back on and ski up.

- For safety reasons it is advisable that no one overtakes within the group, except to overtake a faller who is not injured.

- When skiing individually, each skier should ski at a speed and technique to his or her ability.

- When skiing in formation, the leader sets the speed and technique to suit the whole group.

- By all types of formations, except following in line, each skier should make their own track.

- A fall is liable to cause injury. The leader should ski in such a way so as not to fall, and lead the group down in such a way as to minimise the chance of any of them falling. It is not a piste situation with the ski patrol a few minutes away. Any accident might take a couple of hours to sort out and this may also mean not making it to the hut. If the leader is injured, the responsibility is handed over to the group for the rescue. A very embarrassing situation for the leader.

- The ground rules should be laid out by the leader, in advance, and the group members have the responsibility of keeping to the directions given by the leader.

- Before setting off, the length of the run should be established, with the next stop clearly visible.

- The stops should all be in safe areas.

- The leader generally skis to one side and everyone else to the side and above of the leader. The leader may have to indicate the outside limits of the downhill section.

- Count everyone in at each stop. Make the stop long enough so that every member, even the one to come in last, has a chance to catch their breath and sort their kit out.

A group getting ready for a downhill section.

Which methods to use and when

The method selected depends a lot on the group's ability to ski the snow conditions and on any likely dangers. The following formats are regularly used:

- Formation skiing

- Individual skiing
- Skiing in line behind the leader
- Skiing roped up

Technique points for formation skiing:

- In safe snow/avalanche conditions.
- When you can see everything ahead.
- The leader uses his or her track to mark the outside limits and any danger areas.
- The group ski above and to the side of the leader keeping close to the leader's track.
- Also, when there is no visible danger, the leader may set a track. This to avoid any misunderstanding or possibly to direct the line to the better snow.
- When there is no visible danger the formation can be changed to V-form, or to cross over tracks with a partner.
- The advantages of formation skiing are that the group skis together, the slope is not cut up in every direction, the next group have some fresh snow left to ski in and it gives a very nice optical view when you are looking back.
- It is easier to ski in powder in your own track as the resistance from the snow is constant. Skiing through others tracks brings the skis through a fast - slow - fast system which is not good for your balance.

Formation Skiing

Technique points for individual skiing:

This method is normally used in situations which require more caution on the safety side. It has the disadvantage of being slower than formation skiing.

- In difficult ground and also when it is hard to see from the top.
- In narrow gullies and couloirs.
- As an avalanche precaution when it is not advisable to have the whole group on the slope at the same time.
- On steep slopes with a lot of new snow.
- Constant visual contact must be kept with the person skiing.
- This form has the advantage that the group members do not get in each others way, the snow pack is not unduly weighted and only one person is exposed to the danger at a time.

Individual skiing

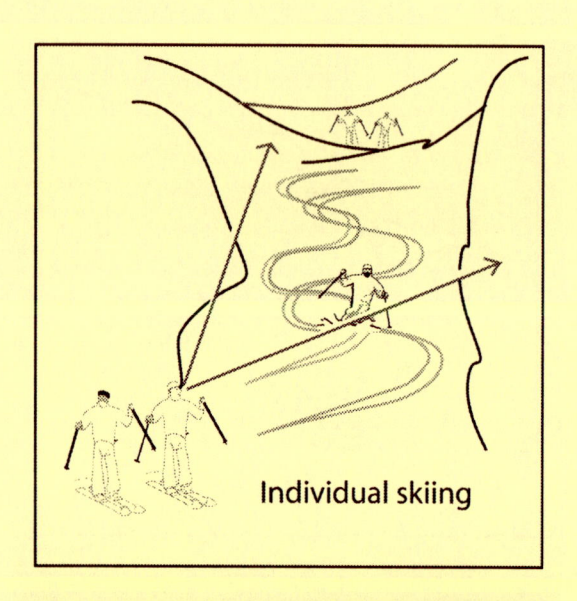

A typical situation where it would be advisable to ski one at a time.

A Complete Guide to Ski Touring and Ski Mountaineering

Technique points for skiing in line behind the leader:

This technique allows the safest descent in adverse conditions.

- Used where there are dangerous passages (crevasses, rocks, drop offs).

- Almost always used in bad visibility.

- Used in difficult snow conditions when the group are not strong skiers.

- The leader skis slowly in front laying a fairly flat track so that it will not be too fast for the people at the back.

- Each turn (normally an uphill stem, or kick turn) is followed by a short traverse.

- The leader makes the track on all turns as wide as possible (not the curve but the width of the track - this might require the leader to stamp the snow down a little).

- In crud conditions the better skiers in the group ski directly behind the leader and ski just above the track of the leader, pushing the snow into the leader's track, thereby making it wider. The weaker members of the group should be in the middle and the strongest skier at the back.

- The group should be sufficiently spaced, to allow everyone stopping time.

- Any stops to regroup should be put in at the end of a flat area and not directly after a turn.

- This method has the advantage that the group can be safely led, every member of the group stays in the safe area, the speed can be controlled by the leader, a good track can be laid for the weaker skiers, the group learn how to pick a good line, and this is also the fastest method of getting a weaker group of skiers from the top to bottom as there is likely to be less falls.

Skiing in line behind the leader

Top tips for the leader:

- Lay the track flat as it will get faster as more people ski it.

- It is also possible to have the group side step or side slip to get over awkward passages - especially in areas where there is no space to put a turn in, or on very steep ground where the consequences of a fall would be a serious slide with likely injury. When doing this, note the way in and out and make sure the skis point in the correct direction. This saves the group having to kick turn on steep ground. Depending on the type of danger you may need the group to come down one at a time or very close to one another. In extreme situations a fixed rope for the group to hold onto is a great confidence booster and increases safety.

5.3 Skiing in avalanche danger areas

The same criteria apply skiing down hill as skiing up hill. As the subject of avalanche is a fairly complex one, we have left it until later in the book.

5.4 Skiing in glaciated areas

Here, as in the chapter on skiing uphill, the ground rules and questions about whether or not to rope up are the same. There are, however, a few extra points that are taken into consideration. They say a lot of good friendships have been broken when skiing roped together downhill, and if you have ever tried it you will know what we mean. It is a difficult technique to master for good skiers, let alone those who are having enough problems coping with the snow on their own. However, do not be tempted to cut out the safety of the rope just because skiing with the rope is a nuisance.

When stopping to regroup on a glacier-keep your distance from the next person.

Technique points skiing without the rope:

- A harness is worn all the time on the glacier.
- Keep your distance from other skiers, about 20m.
- In areas where the crevasses are close together it may be necessary to ski following in line.

- When stopping to regroup, everyone should still keep their distance apart so that the whole group is not standing on the same snow bridge.

- Try to avoid aggressive hard skiing or taking a fall as this puts a lot more weight on any snow bridges that are underneath you.

- An advantage to skiing unroped is that you move over the snow bridges quickly thus minimising the danger.

- Avoid making any turns directly on top of snow bridges (with experience and a little look left and right you can often estimate where the snow bridges might be).

Technique points for skiing with the rope:

There are two types of formation to use here - both have their uses; each providing a different safety purpose. These two types are:

- Following in line of the leader's track.

- Everyone turning at the same time.

Preparing to move off.

Technique points following in line of the leader's track:

This is the technique that should be used if you have to ski roped-up as it offers the most security to the whole group.

- The leader skis at the front and lays a track suitable for the type of terrain and the ability of the group. The speed is quite slow to minimise the danger of pulling one another over.

- The group stay on a tight rope and follow in the leader's track.

- The person at the back can take a couple of coils of rope in their hand to ease the use of the rope. The ski poles can be put in/on the rucksack leaving the hands free for better control of the rope.

- The best ski technique here is the uphill stem turn.

- When stopping, the group stay their distance on the rope.

- If there are any noticeable thin snow bridges, it may be necessary to secure the group members over one at a time.

- For the group members it is often easier to hold the rope in one hand (the rope that is going to the person in front of you), as this helps prevent anyone tripping over it.

- If you have decided to rope-up, it is because you believe it is dangerous. Stay sharp and keep your rope skills in good order in preparation for someone falling in a crevasse.

Technique points for everyone turning at the same time:

This technique should only be used to get over passages where there is no direct danger of falling in a crevasse.

- The leader skis out in front, taking a safe line, and at a pace suitable for the snow conditions and the group's ability.

- The group follow in their own track but in the same line as the leader, all turning at the same time.

- Good communication is required.

- If you use this technique incorrectly in dangerous, steep terrain it can quickly lead to the whole group ending up in the same crevasse and in serious danger.

6 Safety Techniques

Many ski tours comprise of dangerous passages that pass either over rock, ice, or a combination of both. This type of technical terrain, and also glacier, travel will need the use of a rope. Rescue techniques should be practised prior to your departure on a ski tour.

The following pages describe the safety methods required to ski tour and travel whilst using a rope.

6.1 The Rope

The ropes used to both climb and travel on glaciers are known as kern-mantle ropes. They are dynamic and very resilient. The diagram below shows the composition of the ropes, and also the diameters which can now be purchased. Incidentally, the 1 in a circle means that it is a full rope and you can use this rope on its own (single), ½ in a circle means you would need two of these to climb with (double), and is most effective when clipping each rope into separate quickdraws when climbing, the inter-connecting circles (twin) mean you must clip both ropes into the same quickdraws when climbing. For glacier travel a full rope or half rope can be used.

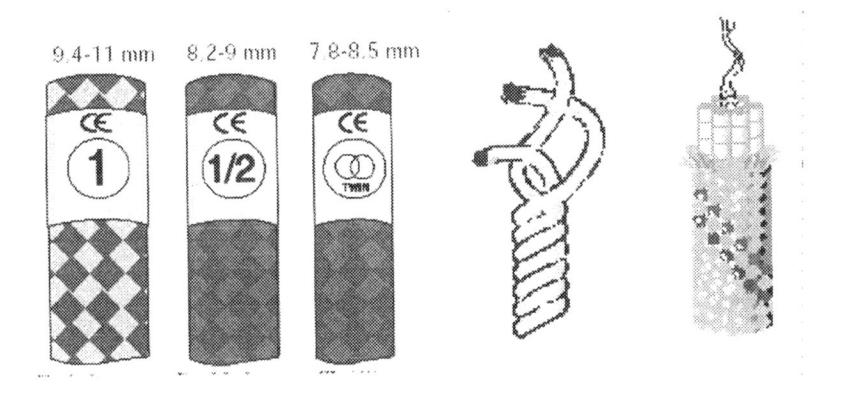

A Complete Guide to Ski Touring and Ski Mountaineering • 83

Duty of Care for Ropes

It is important that the rope is looked after and stored in a dry place and out of direct sunlight whilst not in use. Try to adhere to the rules below:

- Do not stand on the rope with or without crampons.
- Keep out of direct sunlight for long periods.
- If need be wash in lightly warmed water.
- Keep the rope away from oils, acids and other corrosive type fluids.

Basic Technical Safety

The use of ropes whilst ski touring in high mountainous areas requires practise. It is crucial that you have a good working knowledge of the basics prior to your departure into the mountains and that you become familiar with some of the common rescue techniques.

6.2 Knots

Whilst ski touring and ski mountaineering the following knots are widely used:

- Figure 8
- Clove hitch
- Italian Hitch
- Joining two ropes together (Abseil)
- Various prusik knots

6.2.1 Figure 8 knot.

This knot is known in Italy as the Savoy Knot because it appears in the coat of arms of the house of Savoy. It is used whilst ski touring not only because of the fact that it is a very effective knot, but because it can also be undone easily when a heavy load has been put upon it. As with all knots, when tied it is good practice, that another member of the group checks it prior to departure.

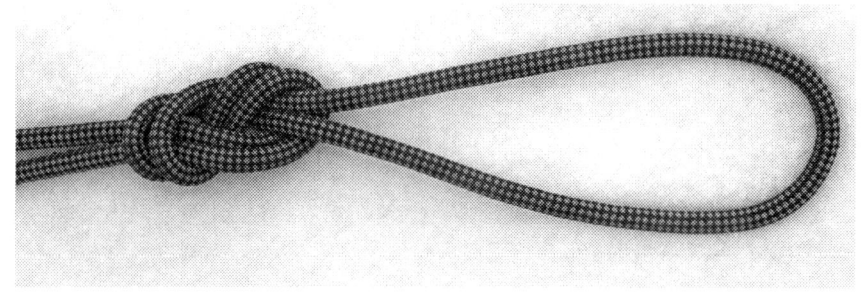

Figure 8 knot

6.2.2 Clove hitch.

The clove hitch is used to secure the climber to a belay point and is also used within the belay itself. It is a very useful knot as it can be adjusted easily.

Clove hitch

A Complete Guide to Ski Touring and Ski Mountaineering

6.2.3 Italian hitch.

The Italian hitch, or munter hitch is a reversible moving knot that can be used in both ascent and descent. It is very quick to tie and, with practice, straightforward to use. One of the most important things with this knot is that the free running rope runs along the back bar of the karabiner so as not to open the gate.

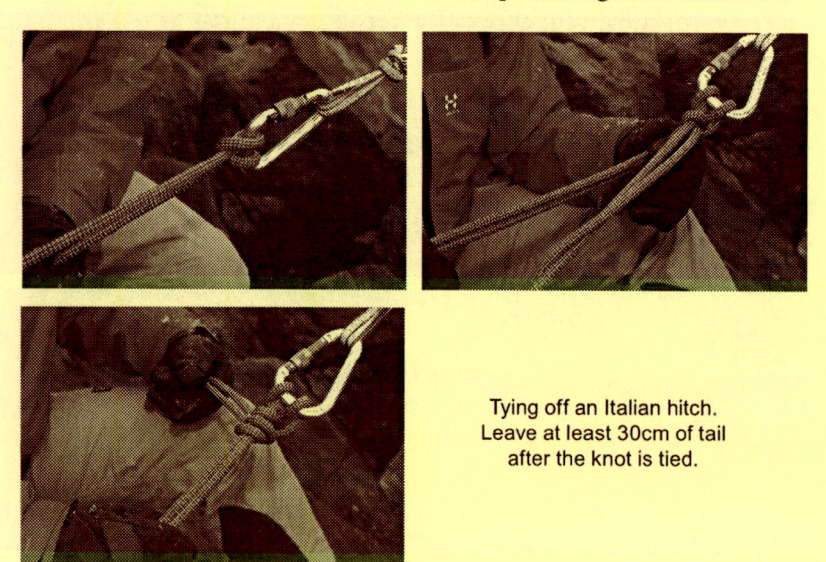

Tying off an Italian hitch.
Leave at least 30cm of tail after the knot is tied.

6.2.4 Joining two ropes together

When joining 2 ropes together, as is often required for an abseil, there are two methods normally used. The first is with the use of an over hand knot. This knot has the advantage that it runs over obstacles well but it is important to leave at least twelve inches of tail sticking out of the knot. It is also good practice to tighten the knot from each strand of rope - this will ensure that the knot is secure. The second method is the fisherman knot. You can use this knot when joining two ropes of the same size or two ropes of different size. By joining two ropes together it will give you double the amount of descent distance which is often very useful if you have to get off the mountain in a hurry.

Joining two ropes together with an overhand knot and a double fisherman.

6.2.5 Various prusik knots

Classic prusik knot

There are various prusik knots that can be used when ski touring. The one shown here is a classic prusik but they can all be used for ascending fixed ropes, in crevasse rescues or climbing rescues, and as self-protection when descending, to list but a few of the uses for this very versatile knot. It has many different uses in many different circumstances.

Top tip:

- When using a classic prusik on crevasse rescue, it is important to ensure the securing bar on the prusik is facing upwards. This will ensure that the knot does not slip when being used.

A classik prusik

French prusik

The French prusik can be used very effectively as an auto block (one which allows the rope to run freely through, but also holds the rope as a back up device) within rescue systems (see the chapter on rescues). The big advantage with this knot is that it will release under pressure.

French prusik

Top Tip:

- When using the French prusik put the prusik loop around the rope a maximum of six and a minimum of four times in order to ensure optimal effect.

6.3 Tying into the harness for climbing

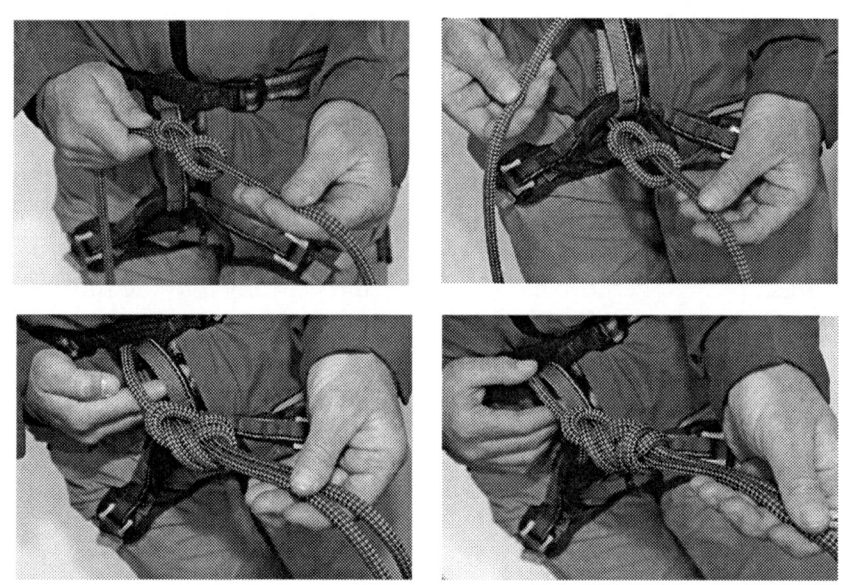

Tie a single figure 8.   Thread the rope through the tie in point. Re-thread the figure 8. Finish the figure 8 off with a fisherman's knot.

6.4 Belays in Snow, Ice and Easy Rock

A very important basis for protecting yourself and your party on Glaciers and on dangerous ground is the understanding of how belays are constructed. Belays are used when climbing in snow, ice and rock as well as for protection when lowering down slopes which cannot be back climbed safely and they are essential in mountain rescue situations.

6.4.1 Belays in Snow

If you require to install fixed points in firn snow, wet glaciers, and on steep slopes which have deep snow conditions, it is important that the correct method of belay is used for the specific type of snow conditions you find yourself in.

Using an ice axe.

Firstly make a small ditch across the falline of the slope. Minimal depth must be the depth of the axe i.e. 50-70 cms. At the axe's balance point make a channel directly down the falline. Place a sling around the balance point secured with a clove hitch. Skis can also be used in the same way by laying the skis together (the bases of the skis must be together to avoid the sharp edges cutting into the sling).

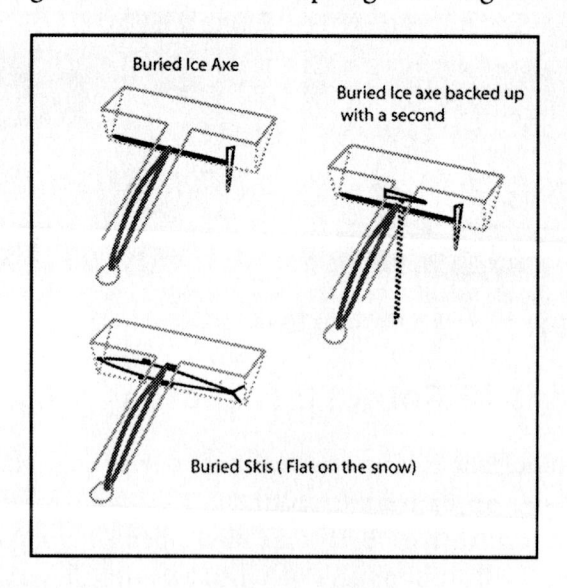

Buried Ice Axe

Buried Ice axe backed up with a second

Buried Skis (Flat on the snow)

6.4.2 Belays in Ice

Fixed points in ice are best constructed using ice screws. The optimal set-up angle is reached by putting the screw in at approximately 100° (vertical to the ice and tilt it back a little). A rough guide to the construction of the belay is to put the first screw in and then the second should be positioned approximately fingers to elbow down and one hand span across - this will prevent the ice failing in both places (dinner plating).

Threads in Ice (Abolako)

The strongest thread to use is an abolako thread. It is constructed by putting the ice screw into the ice at a 45° angle to one another so that the second screw penetrates into the cavity left by the first screw. You now have a "V" in the ice. Once the holes are in place, thread a prusik cord through and tie an over hand knot in the cord to close the loop

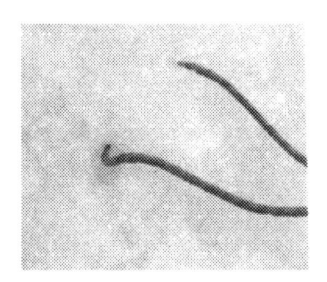

Top tip:

- Ensure the distance between the holes is a minimum of 20cms.

Snow or Ice Bollard

Snow and ice bollards are time consuming to construct but very effective. Both are constructed similarly with the snow bollard being larger - the size of it depending on the texture of the snow. Using an axe, dig a horse-shoe shape in the snow/ice with the fat end at the back. In ice it must be a minimum of 40 cms in diameter and 25 cms deep. The mushroom shape should not meet at the front (it is not a circle). This will ensure that the construction doesn't come away from the rest of the snow or ice pack.

To ensure extra safety in a snow bollard, place an axe at the back in between the rope and the bollard.

6.2.3 Belays in Easy Rock

The ski mountaineer learns to use the rock more effectively with the use of spikes, threads and more natural protection. The ski mountaineer adapts and improvises the techniques learnt in other areas of mountaineering because to carry a complete lead rack whilst ski mountaineering would slow down progress considerably. The following photos show:

- A thread belay in rock.

- A spike belay in rock.

- Using an Italian hitch in a belay system.

Ensure the rope threads through

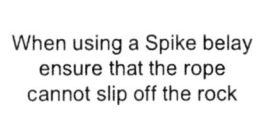

When using a Spike belay ensure that the rope cannot slip off the rock

A Complete Guide to Ski Touring and Ski Mountaineering • 93

The first Karabiner is for your safety. Connect a second Karabiner into the first and ensure that it is behind your clove hitch knot as it might be necessary to take your clove hitch out later (escape from the system).

In some circumstances you will feel happier if you have more than one anchor point in the belay. The chart below shows some safe angles and some dangerous ones.

Angles and the resulting load on the anchors

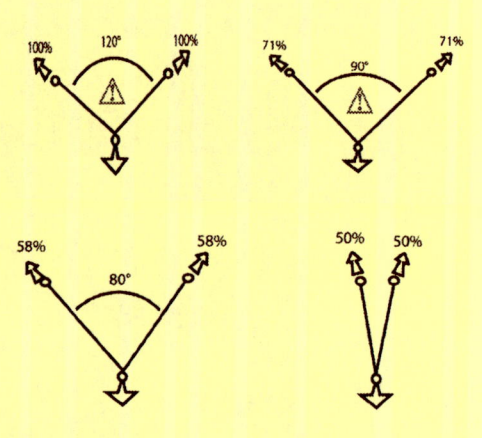

6.5 Use of Belay Devices

Belay devices are generally safe when used correctly but can be dangerous if the basic safety points and correct operating techniques are not adhered to. Ensure that you read the manufacturer's instructions before using the device. One of the most popular types of belay device on the market is an ATC. When you use this device correctly 180° lock off on the dead rope will ensure safety whilst belaying or lowering a climber. An Italian hitch can only be operated from below the system which means that you have to be able to stand in front of it. A device like an ATC on the other hand is best operated when you can stand behind it. As there are so many different devices on the market you must ensure that you are familiar with the usages of the device that you have, both in ascent and descent, before venturing into the mountains.

Top tip:

- Purchase a belay device which will allow you to abseil as well as belay. This cuts out the requirement to carry two devices.

This device will allow you to belay a lead climber in ascent and allow you to abseil. Ensure that 180° are between the live & dead ropes when locking off.

A Complete Guide to Ski Touring and Ski Mountaineering

Top tip:

- When ski touring we must remember that a minimal amount of equipment will be carried. Techniques differ slightly in the Alps to climbing in the UK. Normal safety must always be paramount and not short cut.

6.6 Climbing calls

SITUATION	COMMAND
Lead climber finds a belay and makes safe	SAFE (NAME)
Belayer takes off belay	OFF BELAY (NAME)
Lead climber takes in the slack rope	TAKING IN (NAME)
Rope becomes tight on the Belayer	THAT'S ME (NAME)
*Lead climber puts the Belayer on belay **and checks the belay***	CLIMB WHEN READY (NAME)
Belayer strips out the bottom belay	CLIMBING NOW (NAME)
Lead climber checks the belay	OK (NAME)

After a command shout your climbing partner's name. If others are climbing in the area, this simple task will eliminate confusion.

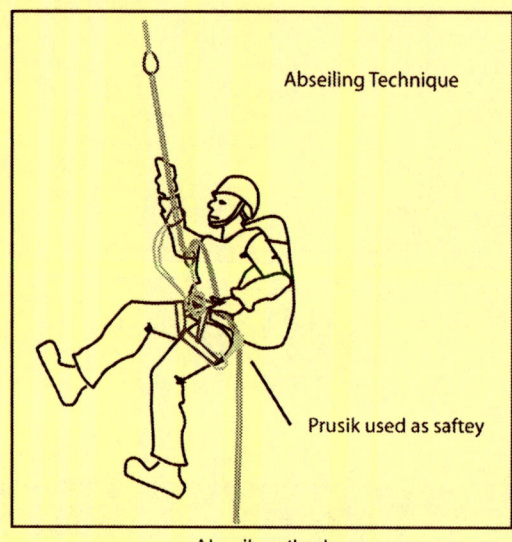

Abseiling Technique

Prusik used as saftey

Abseil method

6.7 Safety on Glaciers

When travelling over glaciated ground, special techniques are required to ensure safety for you and your group. This is not only in ascent but also in descent. The basic principle is that everyone in the group should be tied onto a rope so that no one in the party can fall into a crevasse without being restrained by the other party members. There are four times when you should rope the party together for crossing glaciers:

- When you do not know the glacier.

- When you cannot see anything due to bad visibility.

- When you cannot see the crevasses because they are covered in snow.

- If you are uncertain whether or not to rope up then rope up. You will not be making the wrong decision, but you might be if you decide to go unroped.

The distance should be the same between each person travelling on the rope and this distance should be about 8-12m. How functional the whole system is relies upon the correct behaviour of each individual in the team. Each person should try to ensure that the distance is maintained at all times, even when stops are called for. At no time should the group be stood together as it is possible that they might all be standing on top of a crevasse. Three-person teams are the norm for moving over glaciers, but it is possible to go in pairs if you are heading to do a climb as well, or you can also move in groups of four or five. More people on the rope is generally safer because if the first person falls in a crevasse the others can easily hold the weight and, simply by walking backwards, pull the person back out of the crevasse. Moving uphill it is also fairly easy for the team to hold the leader falling in a crevasse because that person's weight has to pull the other members of the team uphill. Moving downhill requires everyone in the team to stay alert because if the first person in the team falls in a crevasse and the second person trips over and starts sliding as well then it is difficult for the other members of the team to counter that forward movement and hold the fallers.

Overhand knots are used in two man teams

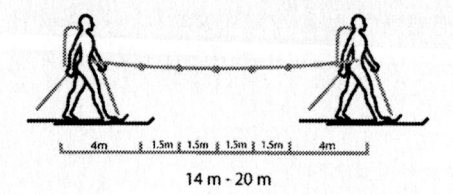

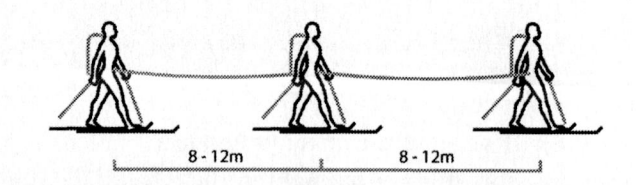

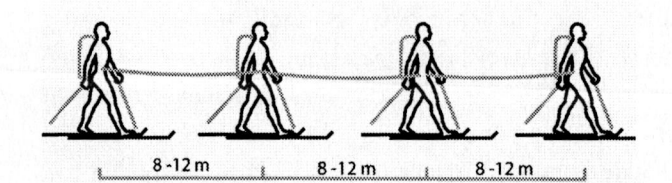

4m | 1.5m | 1.5m | 1.5m | 1.5m | 4m
14 m - 20 m

8 - 12m | 8 - 12m

8 -12 m | 8 -12 m | 8 -12 m

Spare rope is carried in the rucksack from the people at the end of the team.

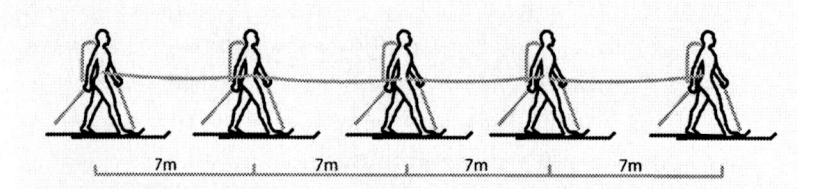

7m | 7m | 7m | 7m

98 • *A Complete Guide to Ski Touring and Ski Mountaineering*

6.7.1 Roping Up Methods

When roping up for the glacier, the rope connects to the harness by a Figure 8 knot into a screw karabiner. Ensure you close the karabiner correctly. A prusik knot can be placed on the rope in preparation for crevasse rescue but modern practice seems to be that you can put it on when you require it. If you are not going to put a prusik knot on the rope, at least make sure that it is close at hand. The middle of the rope is always the start point and the positions of the team members are worked out from here. The spare rope would then be at the ends and this is placed loosely into the rucksack of the team members at either end. An easy way to work out where everyone should be on the rope is to use the spider's web method. The middle person holds the middle of the rope and the two ends. The other members hold the rope and let it slide through their fingers as they walk backwards until the rope is equally divided between each member. It is worth noting that the spare rope at the ends should be long enough to reach the next person and a little more to allow for stretch. The spider's web method allows the rope to be divided equally between the group. We find this method is very quick and ensures equal distance between the group members prior to travel.

Tying onto the rope for movement over glaciers.

A Complete Guide to Ski Touring and Ski Mountaineering

When ski mountaineering, it is possible to move on the glacier as a two-man team. However, for safe movement over glaciers a minimum of three is recommended.

If you have to travel in a team of two it helps to tie overhand knots in the rope between the two members. The idea here is to put drag on the rope if one person falls in the crevasse thus making it easier for the other person to hold the fall. Self-rescues are normally carried out in teams of two because the person holding the faller cannot let the weight off the rope to construct a belay.

7 Clothing and Equipment for Ski-Touring

Clothing should be chosen according to the environment in which you intend to ski. What you wear whilst skiing on piste will differ to what you wear whilst on a tour in the mountains. It is also wise to carry spare clothing to provide warmth when you take a break, when approaching the summit or the windward side of the mountain. Nowadays there is an enormous choice of clothing, covering every conceivable situation, which is designed to fit all shapes and sizes.

Most manufactures offer a wide range of designs. Consider carefully what you require your clothing for to avoid wasting money.

7.1 Fabrics

There are no right or wrongs to what you should wear whilst ski touring. Some fabrics are better in certain situations than others. Cotton is comfortable and absorbs sweat, but it is not hard wearing doesn't dry quickly and doesn't keep you warm. A warm and functional base layer is a key item to wear and essential for protecting from the cold of the outdoors. High performance base layers use a rapid wickering (movement of moisture away from the body) fabric to provide superior performance for all outdoor activities. A choice of weight and styles give perfect options to keep you moving in comfort. Man made fabrics such as polyester and nylon, are hard wearing and dry extremely quickly. If you like tight fitting under garments make sure they stretch. Lycra garments are the stretchiest of all.

Close fitting clothing, particularly fleeces, can be very clammy on extremely hot days and if you're working hard may lead to overheating, which in turn will decrease work output.

Top tips for clothing:

• When choosing trousers for skiing they should have a full length zip, which allows easy use when skis are on the feet. There should also be an internal snow gaiter and preferably braces, which can be worn when ski touring with a rucksack.

• For ski tourers and mountaineers, travelling in environments where their outerwear forms the core of their comfort, safety and survival, a winter outer layer needs to offer comprehensive protection in sub-zero conditions whilst allowing unrestricted movement. Features to improve harsh weather protection include reinforced shoulders and arms, and underarm zips with full storm flap on all openings. A multi panel integral hood to accommodate a helmet and tough, abrasive resistant fabrics are a must. When choosing a jacket it is important that the jacket is made from a waterproof material - either Gore-Tex or a soft shell making sure it has a hood.

Head protection is also very important. Ensure the hat is not too thick, as this can also cause overheating and slow the progress of the tour. Ensure you have ear protection (head band), which will protect against cold winds on an early alpine start..

Gloves (a thin pair) should be worn when ascending. This will also protect your skin if you fall on the snow. Ensure you carry a spare pair for that really cold day. One technical pair should be kept in your rucksack if ski mountaineering.

7.2 Technical equipment for ski touring

There is an abundance of technical equipment available for ski touring. Correct research into the type and difficulty of the tour will determine what equipment is needed. Minimum equipment that should be carried on every tour is: rope, transceiver, shovel, probe, Harscheisen, skins. Without these, all simple variation trips (off piste, steeps and deeps) turn into an adventure with no calculated risk. The basic equipment allows ski touring on glaciated terrain or in the mountains to become safer. For ski mountaineering expect to carry more technical alpine equipment, for example crampons, ice axe, assorted rack of rocks on wires, pitons, and helmet.

All equipment used whilst ski touring should be of the highest standard. Ensure that it has been approved by UIAA, DIN or CE. All of these abbreviations can be found somewhere on the equipment.

Below is some technical equipment that you may carry whilst ski mountaineering

Rucksack

A rucksack should fit comfortably. It shouldn't exceed the width of the body, as this will impede movement when rock climbing. A 35 litre rucksack should be large enough to ski tour/mountaineer. Ensure that you can fit all your equipment inside as having anything dangling outside will cause you problems.

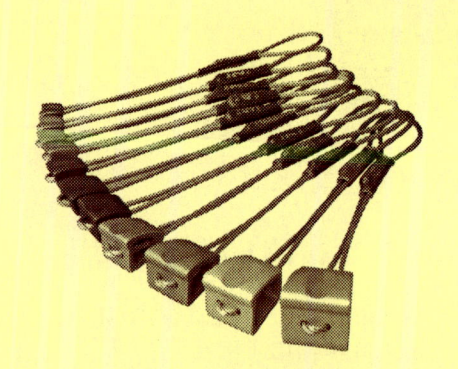

Wallnuts

Colour coordinated for ease of size recognition, the walnut is a classic piece of protection cleverly shaped to help protect difficult passages.

Colour coordinated wallnuts

Crampons

Used correctly, crampons are vital to safe winter walking and mountaineering. The wrong combination of boot and crampon is, however, potentially very dangerous so before you consider your choice of crampon you must first establish the suitability and grading of your boots.

The boot and crampon grading system are designed to protect against incompatible combinations. For example, while it is practical to use B3 graded (fully stiffened) boots with any crampon, it is not safe to use a B1 (modestly stiff hill walking boot) boot with anything stiffer than C1 (flexible) grade crampon.

C1 Generally 8-10 point crampon where the toe and heel sections are connected by a flexible bar.

C2 Generally 10-12 point crampon with the heel and toe sections joined by either an adjustable bar or simple hinge.

C3 Usually 12 points, but sometimes with a mono point at the front. C3 crampons are fully rigid along their entire length.

A C2 crampon.

Ice axe / walking / technical

There are many axes on the market. You should choose a fairly lightweight axe which allows you to comfortably travel on glaciers and climb steep terrain. Here are some examples (you will see that the non technical axes have a straighter adze and pick, whereas the technical axes are more angled):

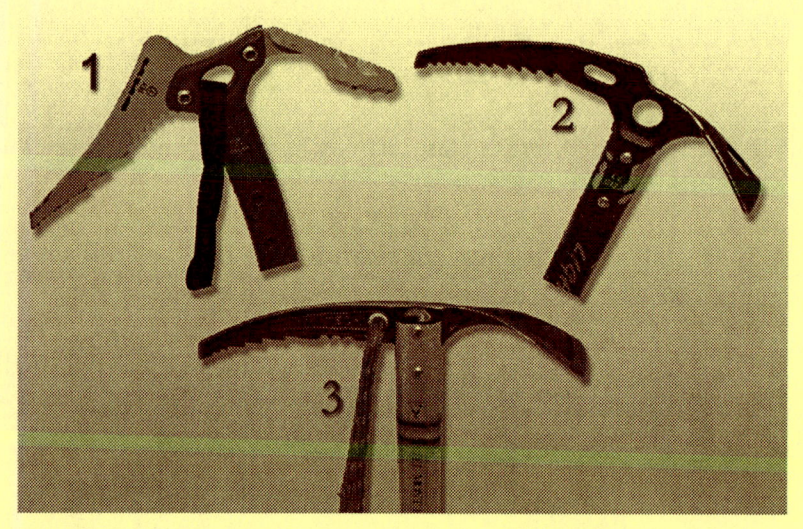

1=Climbing axe. 2 and 3=more suitable for walking

Karabiners

Karabiners should always be used in conjunction with the manufacturer's user guide. Never cross load them and always ensure they are correctly fastened when in use.

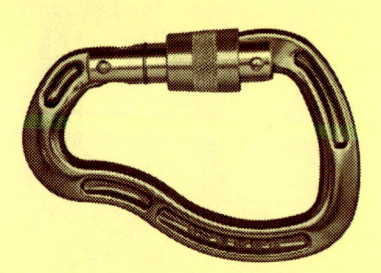

A screw gate type karabiner offers good safety.

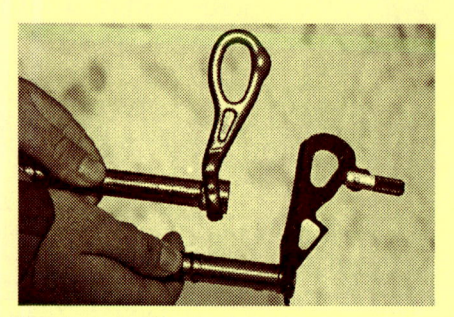

Ice screws

Ice screws can be purchased at different lengths depending on the level of activity undertaken. Try and buy express ice screws as they are quicker to put into ice.

Two ice screws.

Harness

A comfortable harness is an essential part of your experience in the mountains. It will allow you to climb with complete freedom and easy access to your gear.

A good fit is essential for both safety and comfort. Adjustable harnesses have increased in popularity in recent years as they can be adjusted to ensure both security and comfort.

A comfortable fit and adjustable leg loops are important.

Basic alpine harnesses are generally unpadded. The harness will ensure that you can adjust both leg loops and waist belt when crampons have been fitted to boots and whilst wearing skis.

Rope

A half rope is sufficient for glacier travel, however there are specific ropes on the market for ski touring and glacier travel. These ropes usually weigh about 45-50g/m which keeps the weight that you carry relatively light.

Prusik

Prusik cord is important when travelling on glaciated ground as it is used with crevasse rescue (see rescue chapter). A prusik cord has many uses and it is recommended to carry a minimum of two in 5mm diameter. Because of their variation of use people tend to carry a selection of lengths and diameter.

Slings

Dynema slings are very useful as they can be used as prusik's, to thread ice screws, or to extend prusik's in some cases to give just a few examples. It is recommended to carry 2x8ft and 1x16ft which will allow you flexibility in all circumstances.

7.3 Minimum equipment required to ski tour

The absolutely minimum equipment required to ski tour is described in detail below:

Transceiver

The Transceiver is one of the most important pieces of technical equipment carried by the ski tourer, ski mountaineer. When one is proficient with its usage there is little error to be made. It is very important that you set up various practice scenarios at the beginning of the ski season. This ensures no time is wasted when needed in a real life situation. Modern electronic transceivers work on a frequency of 457 KHz. When using the transceiver in very windy conditions the use of ear phones is an advantage.

A transceiver held in search position

(Usage of the transceiver can be found in the avalanche chapter.)

Top tip

- Mobile telephones can interfere with the signal that the Transceiver transmits. To ensure that your transceiver functions correctly, keep your mobile switched off until it is required.

Avalanche shovel and probe

When someone is the victim of an avalanche and isn't wearing a Transceiver it is important that they are searched for using an avalanche probe (details of searching for buried victims can be found in the avalanche chapter). An avalanche probe should, when assembled, be stable and should be marked with different colours. The shovel should be lightweight but stable enough to be used in hard packed snow should you need to dig a shelter for a rest or to overnight. Think of the shovel as a multi purpose tool.

Navigation Equipment

For navigation when ski touring and when skiing variables a good topographical map in a scale of 1:25,000 is suitable. Maps produced by the German Alpine Association & Austrian Alpine Association have ski tour routes marked on them. The altimeter is used in conjunction with the map and is invaluable when visibility is poor. The compass should have a romer scale on it for 1:50,000 and 1:25,000 maps, a magnifying area, and a scale in degrees or mils.

(Navigation is covered in greater depth in the navigation chapter.)

Skis

Skis have changed immensely over the past 5 years. Alpine skis are being used more and more. Powder skis, free ride skis and even Telemark. Prior to purchase you should gather as much information as possible about the skis and how you intend to use them.

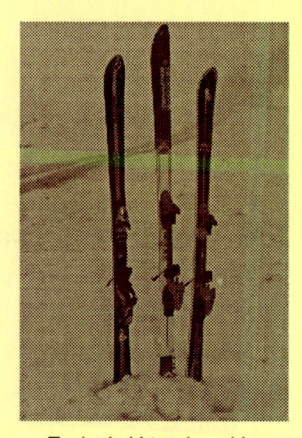

Typical ski touring skis

Touring bindings and Harscheisen

Touring bindings have become highly developed in recent years. In particular, the weight and function of these bindings have become increasingly advanced. It is important that there is a heel raise on the binding which will help when ascending steeper terrain.

The binding pivots at the front to allow a smooth ascent of steep slopes.

The Harscheisen (ski crampon) can be easily fitted to the ski binding. This is used when the terrain is icy and the snow conditions are compact. Harscheisen are designed for specific bindings and come in different sizes to match binding sizes. Check that your harscheisen fit your binding before you set off on tour.

Ski touring boot and piste boot

For off piste skiing and short ski tours without long and difficult sections, the normal alpine ski boot will suffice. When ski touring over several hours with continued long and technical sections, with the possible expectation of climbing some rock steps, correct ski touring boots are to be recommended in every case. When more difficult terrain is involved, the use of correct boots is the only choice to make, and these should allow you to change the boot into uphill or downhill mode quickly (walk & ski mode). Be certain that your boot accepts your crampon choice.

There are many ski touring boots on the market. Get good advice from ski shops and ensure they fit properly.

Ski touring ski poles

The ski pole used when ski touring is a 2 or 3 piece telescopic pole - one which can be collapsed when the hands are needed to climb a short section of difficulty. The stick can also be extended and used as an avalanche probe and as a splint for an injured arm or leg.

Top tips

- When conditions are very cold it is important to have the hand which is on the ski pole lower than the elbow, this will allow the blood to keep the fingers warm.

- Non telescopic ski poles can be used for easier ski tours where no climbing is involved.

Ski skin

The fur on the skin prevents the ski slipping backwards when on steep terrain and also when touring on hard compact snow. For a perfect functioning skin, the skin should be re-glued when the original glue becomes non-adhesive (once per season). Use correct ski glue – coltex or black diamond.

Top tip

- To re-glue the skin get a brown paper bag, place the bag on the skin (glued side), run an iron over the skin (glued side) peel off the paper, and now apply the new glue.

Sunglasses and goggles

Sun glasses should be worn wherever possible. Purchase a pair which has a protection filter of 3000 UVB or above. Ensure the light doesn't come in from the sides or bottom of the lense, especially when travelling over glaciated terrain. For windy days, when snow could blow inside the glasses, it is a must to have a pair of quality goggles.

First aid pack

The first aid kit should be extensive enough to adhere to the needs of the group when in the mountains. It helps when everyone carries their own small blister and plaster kit.

A Complete Guide to Ski Touring and Ski Mountaineering

8 Practical Avalanche Information

Avalanches represent the major natural threat in the Alpine regions. Protecting villages can be costly, but as knowledge improves it is, in theory, a fairly straight forward process. For ski tourers, on the other hand, it is a bigger problem. The popularity of ski touring is on the increase and people are heading out into the mountains in ever increasing numbers, sometimes with little knowledge of the dangers involved. The local inhabitants and the majority of the tourists and piste skiers are safe in as much as the authorities know where and when the avalanches are likely to occur and can consequently put out the correct warnings. As well as that, the avalanches in these sort of cases are known hot spots and the authorities can clear these areas in plenty of time by closing roads or ski areas. The tourers, however, are heading into the areas where avalanches are likely to occur. The same warnings are there for the ski tourers but these warnings are sometimes ignored and other times simply not understood. The chart below shows the general trend in recent avalanche accidents and one can see clearly that tourers represent the larger percentage of the chart. The aim of this chapter is to try and cut down this trend by improving your knowledge of avalanches, how they happen, why they happen and when they are likely to happen, thereby improving the safety of you and your companions.

Avalanche Statistics

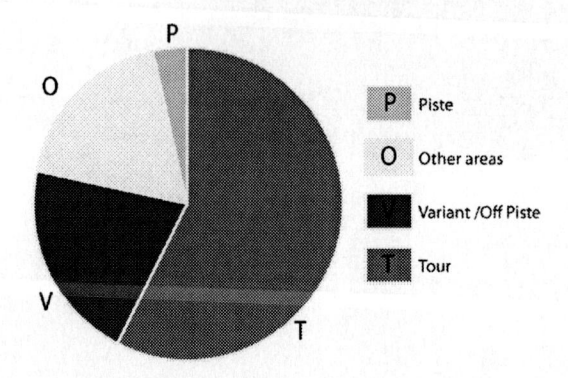

P	Piste
O	Other areas
V	Variant / Off Piste
T	Tour

8.1 Avalanche types

There are 2 main types of avalanches:

a. The slab avalanche is the most dangerous for the skier. This avalanche has a very wide fracture area and it can fracture at 300m per second.

b. The loose snow avalanche, on the other hand, originates from a single point and is normally self release.

Within these two categories there are other descriptions which are important to know. An avalanche can either be:

a. Surface is where it slides on one of its own layers or full depth where the whole snow pack will slide.

b. It can be dry or wet. Wet slides tend to be later in the season when the sun has been out longer. Wet tends also to slide on shallower angles than dry.

c. It can be unconfined as in an open slope or it can be channelled, as in a gully.

d. It can move along the ground or it can move through the air, as in an airborne powder avalanche.

Avalanches can happen on most slopes.

8.2 Snow

It is not essential to understand everything in great detail about snow crystals in order to make a sensible avalanche prediction, but some understanding of falling snow will help put the overall picture together.

When snow falls it falls in different shapes and sizes, depending on what is happening in the higher atmosphere. These shapes have a variety of different cohesive abilities to other crystals. The crystals are liable to change shape as the temperature rises or the wind becomes stronger.

The most important information about new fallen snow

Powder snow has a very distinct V-cut crystal form, in the air, and falls with low temperatures. Because there is little moisture content this crystal is light, and very loose, and is difficult to make a snow ball with. If new snow falls without the presence of wind it is not too dangerous.

Top tips

- On steep ground, loose snow avalanches can occur.
- When wind is present it will immediately bind the snow, even powder snow. This is very dangerous and soft wind slab avalanches are likely to occur

Slushy snow is moist new snow and falls in big flakes with mild temperatures. It is heavy because of its high moisture content and it settles very quickly.

Top tips

- On steep ground it is possible to have a build up of wet loose snow avalanches and also slab avalanches.

Hail, commonly known as graupel, falls through moist air and builds as an ice crystal. Water droplets stick to the crystal on its way to the earth and form this rounded shape. This type of crystal normally comes with a cold front. This type of snow, when on the ground, looks like ball bearings. This means that if new snow falls on top of it, it will have a perfect sliding layer. Be aware.

Riming and Hoarfrost. Riming is formed when droplets of super cooled water impinge on any object in their path. This type can be found on the side of fence posts and is a good indicator of wind direction. The rime formation points into the wind. Hoarfrost is a bright, sparkling crystal which can be found on, above or even below the snow surface. It requires cold clear nights. The snow surface is cooled by losing air to the atmosphere, and any water vapour condenses onto the snow crystals forming a great, crispy surface to ski on.

The snow crystals are subjected to metamorphism which happens from the very first moment the snow crystal is formed. This metamorphism has a massive effect upon the snow pack thus increasing/decreasing the dangers of avalanches. Once the snow lands on the ground it is subject to three different types of metamorphism. These are:

- Equi-temperature metamorphism
- Kinetic growth or temperature gradient metamorphism
- Melt freeze metamorphism

Equi-temperature is the most common of the three. The warmer the temperature the faster this process happens. New snow crystals which fall in the traditional star form gradually lose their shape from the tips and increase their size from the middle, eventually ending up in a roundish sort of ball. These crystals generally bond together well making a fairly safe layer. When the temperature stays cold this process will be delayed, thereby increasing the amount of days of good powder skiing but at the same time maintaining the danger level.

Kinetic growth is common in very cold temperatures over longer periods. The ground normally stays at about freezing point. This, in contrast to the surface temperature, is quite warm. This warm air rises through the snow pack and any moisture sticks to the snow crystals on route. These crystals form into cup shapes and increase in size. This is commonly known as depth hoar, cup crystals, or becker crystals. The big danger here is that these crystals are very fragile and do not bond very well with anything around them.

The larger the temperature gradient, the faster the crystal transforms. Depth hoar can also build in intermediate layers within the snow pack when large temperature differences are present.

Top tips

- A drop in the temperature and a thin snow layer (big temperature falls) will accelerate the danger of depth hoar formations.
- Low snowfall at the beginning of winter and long cold spells without precipitation increases the likelihood of depth hoar forming.

Melt freeze is fairly straightforward; it is more of a late season system as it requires sunshine and warm temperatures followed by cold temperatures. This would be the spring sun that melts the snow followed by the cold nights which freezes it. This type of snow is very stable when in its frozen state. When in its melted state it is dangerous. This is a common feature of afternoon avalanches in spring time, and if the hut guardian is rushing to get you out of the hut for an early start it is probably this that he is concerned about.

8.3 Factors that influences avalanche formation

There are always four primary factors in direct context to avalanches. The problem is that all four of these primary factors vary constantly but should generally be assessed together, and not individually, if you want to get an accurate overall assessment of the avalanche situation.

These factors are:

- The snow pack
- The weather
- The terrain
- The people

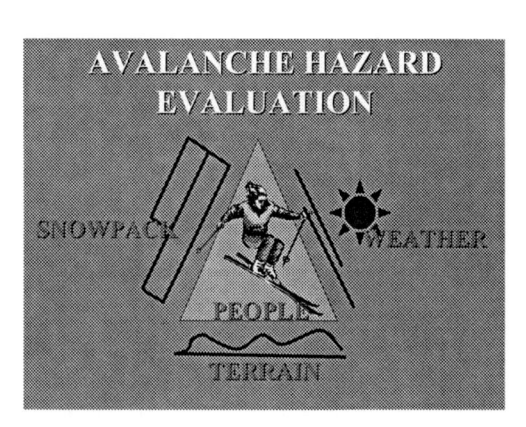

A Complete Guide to Ski Touring and Ski Mountaineering

8.3.1 The snow pack

The snow pack is seen as a layer cake with each layer having different ingredients. These ingredients are hard old snow, new power snow, granules, hail stones or graupel, crystal size, temperature of the layers, moisture of the layers, and the size of the crystals.

Snow pack construction

With some knowledge and experience one can recognise what has been happening to the snow pack over the winter, how the weather has affected it, and how the snow pack has built up.

The following factors have an effect on the snow pack construction:

- Precipitation (snow, rain)
- Wind
- Temperature (cold, warm, solar radiation)
- Structure of the ground
- Other influences (i.e. sand transported in upper air streams)
- Skiers (is the slope skied frequently/infrequently)
- Exposure to the sun (direct influence from the sun)
- Height of the slope (direct influence from the sun)
- Is the slope windward or a Lee aspect

It is important to measure the criteria of each layer on its own merits (new and old contact between the layers). The fundamental criterion is that every layer can change its composite and be regarded as a possible sliding surface. The critical layers are:

- Loose snow (as in a surface hoar which has been snowed over)

- The layer between old and new snow
- The contact between depth hoar and whatever lies above it
- Ice layers
- The connection between soft and hard layers

8.3.2 The weather

The weather plays an important role in the build up of avalanches. It influences the avalanche danger directly and continuously, both positively or negatively

The common negative reasons are:

- New snow with wind. Wind at 30 km/h will move snow to other areas
- Sudden temperature rise
- New snow falling on the top layer which is crusty (creates a sliding surface)

New snow

The stronger the snowfall the more likelihood there is of avalanches building up. As well as this, the overall amount of new snow within a period of time is important. If there is a heavy snowfall then the new snow cannot bond fast enough with the snow pack and eventually the weight of the new snow will cause it to slide.

Critical amounts

- New snow depth of more than 30cm
- New snow of over 2cm per hour.

Other observations

- Wind strength
- Temperature
- Old snow layer
- How often the slope has been descended

Top tips:

- 10-15 cms of new snow in conjunction with high winds can cause slab avalanches.

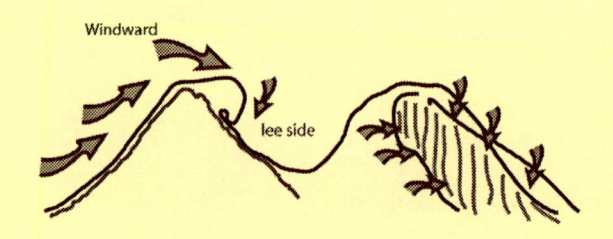

Wind moves snow from the windward side and deposits it on the lee side

The effects of wind

UNFAVOURABLE CONDITIONS	FAVOURABLE CONDITIONS
• Winds stronger than >30km/h • Drop in temperature • A bad bonding between the old and new snow layers i.e. – ice, freeze melt, surface hoar • Angles over 30° • Hillside rarely skied	• Light winds • Temperature under 0°c before the new snow began to fall • Hillside used often

The wind has been named, rightly so, as the master builder of avalanches.

How to judge the wind and how high and low winds are distinguished.

High winds are recognizable at the top of high clouds (lenticular formations). They generally indicate high storms.

Ground winds are directly influenced by the relief of the terrain. They are often in a totally different direction to the high winds.

Wind speeds vary depending on the type of obstacles they meet. The mountains channel winds through narrow valleys or squeeze the winds between ridges and the high winds.

The most potential slab avalanches originate through wind effect or shortly after a snowfall. The loose snow is deposited to the lee side of the slopes (slab avalanche danger) leaving a wind blasted aspect on the windward side. However, this doesn't mean that suspected avalanche danger should be counted out on the windward side. You must exercise caution on steep slopes, in bowls and in gullies.

What's more, in times of good weather, wind in higher regions of the mountains can deposit large amounts of snow.

Top tips:

- Snow cornices at summits, ridges and on spurs are sure signs of snow being moved around by wind.

The wind strength mixes the loose snow and old snow and deposits it in different areas depending on the relief of the terrain.

Temperature

The snow and avalanche situation is influenced massively by the complex interactions of the temperature. The effects of a constant heat exchange have varying effects on the individual layers within the snow pack.

Influence on the snow temperature

Radiation: Solar radiation from the sun can affect the upper layers of the snow pack. This can be seen when small snow balls roll down the slope, melt freeze, or in the build up of surface hoar. The consequence of the solar radiation on the snow pack affects different aspects of slope throughout the season. The influence of this radiation is shown in the chart below. In early winter, on slopes of the same steepness but of different aspects, it takes longer on some slopes to achieve the same settling effect.

EXPOSURE	*PERIOD*
South facing	1 day
East facing	2-3 days
North West to North East facing	13 days

Effects of the Temperature

- Fast and massive warming of the snow pack raises the danger within the snow pack very quickly.

- Slow and steady warming of the snow pack causes a continuous settling within the various layers.

- Continuous low temperatures preserve dangers within the snow pack.

- The effect of cooling the snow hardens moist and heavy snow thus helping settling.

- The danger degree in the early winter is usually parallel to the suns heat. The temperature fluctuations over the day have an effect only 10-30 cm deep on the upper layers, according to snow texture.

- The snowfall border is approximately 300m under the zero degree isotherms. If it is snowing at 1000m with an air temperature of 1.5°, then we can expect 0° at around 1300m.

Rain represents an important avalanche factor. Through the extra moisture within the snow pack it forces the loose layers onto the more stable ones and lubricates any possible sliding layers. When the whole snow pack becomes saturated the whole snow pack can avalanche, known as full depth avalanche.

Top tip

- Wet snow avalanches can release in any aspect of slope and on almost any angle of slope.

8.3.3 The Terrain

The ground relief is a very important factor when discussing avalanche prone slopes. It takes experience to read the ground (which is often covered by large amounts of snow) well in both ascent and descent.

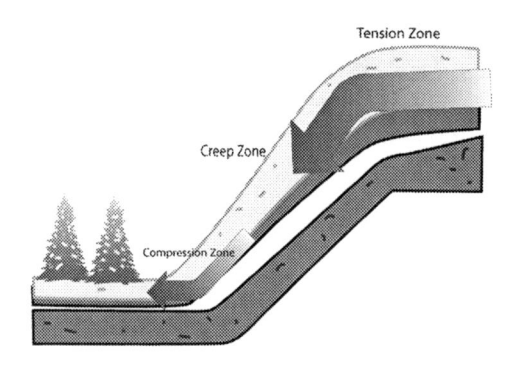

The ground angle and slope are important factors when considering avalanches

Angle of slope

The angle of the slope can be an avalanche trigger. The most common angle for slab avalanches is 30° – 45°, however wet snow can slide on an angle under 20°. On slopes steeper than 45° it is difficult for slabs to form as the snow normally slides off during the snowfall period.

To recognise the critical angle of a slope, the ski tour and movement on the ground should be well planned. When planning the tour, the steepness from the topographical map 1:25,000 can be determined on the basis of the distance between contour lines. 100m height gained on 7mm distance indicates a 30° angle, for example.

Other examples

8mm on the map	-	27°
7mm	-	30°
6mm	-	34°
5mm	-	39°
4mm	-	45°

These determined average values are rounded up.

On the ground the angle can be determined by using an inclometer which can be found on some compasses. When on the ground, you should practise using these tools and also practise the ski stick method indicated below. As a rough guide, if the vertical pole and the horizontal pole are touching handle to handle and the ends are on the snow then the angle is about 45°. When the horizontal pole is halfway down the vertical then the angle is about 28°.

Top tips

- Rocky hillsides are steeper than 40°.

- Moraine slopes are approximately 40° steep.

- In couloirs and gullies the side walls can be steeper than 60°

- Ensure you know what angle of slope you will be travelling on during the tour and watch out for the hot spots.

The land form can develop hot spots within prone avalanche slopes but can also hinder the development of avalanches. Slopes that have a lot of bumps and dips will slow down the speed of avalanches. On the other hand, slopes which are smooth and have grass on the surface will enhance the speed of the slide.

When talking about convex and concaved slopes we must understand where the tension is building up on them.

Using the ski poles to work out the angle of the slope.

Top tips

- Convex land form is generally dangerous at the top, as the snow pack is under so much tension from below. Also, be aware of the bottom of convex slopes as that is where the snow will collect if the slope avalanches.

- Concaved land forms compression spots and will normally be visible. Be aware of possible catchment areas if the slope is loaded.

Vegetation

The vegetation can be an avalanche factor. It will either help to hold the snow in place or it will allow the snow to slide easily. Long grass, for example, is a good sliding layer. Small trees which are fairly spread out hold air around their bases but do not necessarily hold the snow in place. Some vegetation lying just under the surface (old tree stumps) can also be quite dangerous for the skier.

Top tips

- Dense forest with young trees prevents avalanche build up. In a well spaced-out forest the danger is increased.

- Shrub vegetation is only a hindrance and loose snow avalanche can form. It can also hinder the descent of skiers.

Top tips

- Wet snow avalanches can release in any aspect of slope and on any angle of slope.

8.3.4 People

People can be avalanche triggers. If a member of your party cannot ski in control on steep slopes they will become a problem. Skiing in control, whilst descending unknown terrain, is a key point to remember. If someone falls, the weight of that person is multiplied by 10. This extra weight penetrates through the snow pack in every direction. Also, skiing too aggressively can cause problems. Be gentle when turning on steep descents. The ski tourer is someone who moves willingly around the mountains in winter with an understanding (or sometimes without an understanding) of the dangers and risks involved. In order for the ski tourer to move responsibly through the mountains he/she should observe and have an understanding of the following points:

People can be the avalanche trigger.

- Knowledge of weather and the snow pack
- The ability to navigate
- Understand route selection
- Be able to asses their own ability

8.4 Snow pack examinations

There are a few tests which can be carried out on the snow pack to check the stability, however, it must be noted that these tests cannot be taken alone; other factors must be taken into account, for example, weather, snowfall and temperature. These tests are complex and act as additional information to your avalanche report. It is important to gain as much information about the snow pack at a similar aspect and angle of slope to that of your tour.

8.4.1 Snow profile

A snow profile gives information about the construction of the different snow layers. It shows possible hot spots within the snow pack, i.e.

layers with sliding properties. To do a snow profile you firstly have to dig a pit and smooth off the front - how deep you dig depends on how much you want to know. You will get all the information when you dig to the ground, but this could be 3m and not very realistic. You certainly have to dig deep enough to find the layers that you think might be suspect. Once you have your pit, run your finger down the profile from top to the bottom, you will feel the different layers. You must determine how safe each layer is within the snow pack by conducting a simple test on each layer to establish how hard each layer is. A very hard layer next to a very soft layer would not be a good result.

Testing the hardness of the snow pack.

Hard	Condition of snow	Object used
1	Very soft	fist
2	Soft	4 fingers
3	Medium	1 finger
4	Hard	Pen
5	Very hard	Knife
6	Compact ice	

The different layers can be tested for hardness and stability by using the table above.

There are special symbols used internationally to indicate the type of snow crystals in the snow pack. By using a magnifying glass you can relate the symbols to the snow crystals and identify which crystals are less likely to bond together. Earlier in the chapter we mentioned, for example, that cup crystals are not a good bonding crystal.

8.4.2 Symbols used when conducting a snow profile

+ +	New snow crystal approx 7mm diameter
⋌ ⋌	First stages of metamorphism approx 2mm diameter
• •	Rounded granules approx 1 mm diameter
▫ ▫	Angulated grains with flat sides approx 1.5-3mm diameter
^ ^	Cup crystals approx 2-5 mm diameter
∘ ∘	Rounded grains formed by freeze melt approx 1-3 mm diameter
<u>V V</u>	Hoar layer
<u>O O</u>	Melt Hoar
——	Ice layer

8.4.3 Norwegian Shovel Test

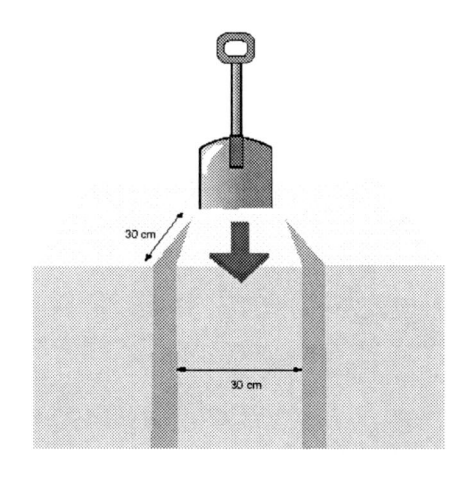

The shovel test is a test to establish where the snow pack is at its most vulnerable. This test will confirm your assessment of where the sliding layers are. It also gives you information about the cohesive layers within the snow pack. The shovel test takes about 10 mins to perform.

With the shovel test you can easily work out a scale of one to five to give you a result to your findings. If the layer comes away as you are putting your shovel into the snow then it is a very dangerous situation. If you are heaving with all your might and nothing is happening then it is fairly safe. The scales in the middle are the ones which require good judgement. When you do this test be careful that the shovel does not go between two layers, as there is a tendency to try to lever the layer free and this will only give you a false reading.

Equipment needed:

Shovel

10 mins approximately

8.4.4 Rutschblock

The Rutschblock is a similar test to the shovel test - more accurate, but also more time consuming. This test is well worth doing on every aspect on your first day in a new area. You could then follow this up by monitoring the daily changes with a shovel test. As with all the tests it only gives you a result from one specific point and only an indication of what it might be like in similar areas.

To dig your rutschblock you dig out a pit 2m across the front, 1.5m back and full depth. The trench at the sides needs to be wide enough to walk into. Once the block has been dug you then use a length of cord to saw down the back of the block so that you have a free standing block held only by the attachment at the bottom. You are now ready to commence your test. A skier moves carefully onto the top end of the block and steps both skis over the line that you cut through, so that he is standing totally on the block. The following actions and values should be recorded:

Stepping on to the rutschblock

1. The block collapses and slides when you are cutting it.
2. The block collapses when the skier steps onto it.
3. The skier flexes his knees and without jumping puts as much weight on the skis as possible.
4. The skier jumps up and lands on the same spot.
5. The skier jumps and lands on the same spot a second time.
6. The skier jumps but lands slightly further down the block or it is also possible to take the skis off and try jumping on the same spot.

Steps 1, 2, and 3 are dangerous on a similar angle, aspect and altitude.

Steps 4 and 5 could give you local instability on similar slopes.

Step 6 shows a low risk of avalanche danger.

The lower and higher results are normally easy to decide and the ones in the middle are those which require some experience. If you are in any doubt then interpret the results as more dangerous and do not assume that it is safe. Your experience will eventually build up so that your decisions are more accurate.

Equipment needed:

Shovel

Prusik cord

20-30 mins approximately

8.5 How to make your decision

When ski touring, it is unlikely that you will have a rucksack full of scientific equipment to help you make a decision on whether it is safe to cross the slope or not. In spite of this, some method of evaluating the situation based on your experience is required. If you always base your decisions on your own experience and not that of another group then you will always be correct. I have often heard people say: 'the guide crossed so it must be safe'. The guide has a different experience level and also there may be other criteria within the guide's group or within the guide's considerations that you are not aware of. Your own experience level will improve over the years and consequently your ability to make decisions closer to the limit will also improve. When considering whether to go or not I normally find that the following three questions help significantly:

Question Number	Question	Considerations	Answer	Result
One	Could the slope avalanche?	1. Slope angle 2. Ground cover 3. Slope altitude 4. Slope aspect 5. Time of day 6. Temperature 7. Which slopes are above me?	Yes = No = I do not know =	Go on to question two Carry on with the tour Turn round and go back
Two	Is the slope likely to avalanche?	1. Avalanche report 2. Snow profile 3. Rutsch block test 4. Warning signs 5. Wind deposited area	Yes = No = I do not know =	Go on to question three Carry on with the tour but think about taking extra precautions Turn round and go back
Three	What will happen to me if the slope does avalanche?	1. Amount of snow 2. Width of avalanche 3. Likely depth of avalanche 4. Length of run out 5. Any vertical drop offs 6. Any obstacles in the avalanche path?	Minimal risk. Even if the slope avalanches there is not enough snow. The run out is short. High risk. A lot of depth, long run out, dangerous drop off. I do not know (bad visibility and cannot see the dangers, or lack of knowledge) =	Take the necessary precautions and cross the slope one at a time. Turn round and go back. Turn round and go back.

A Complete Guide to Ski Touring and Ski Mountaineering

As well as the above chart you should have taken the local avalanche forecast into consideration. There is a European norm for avalanche reports on a scale of one to five so that even if you do not understand the language you will still understand what the numbers relate to. This is shown in the chart below:

EUROPEAN AVALANCHE RISK SCALE

Degree of risk	Snow pack suitability	Avalanche probability	Effects on traffic lines and residential areas/ recommendations	Effects on off piste skiers/ recommendations
1 Low	The snow pack is generally well bonded and stable.	Likely to be triggered off by high additional loads ** on only a very few steep extreme slopes. Only small spontaneous avalanches possible.	No risk of avalanches.	Virtually no restriction for back country and downhill skiing
2 Moderate	The snow pack is moderately well bonded on some * steep slopes, otherwise generally well bonded.	Likely to be triggered off by high additional loads ** mainly on the steep slopes indicated. Large spontaneous avalanches not expected.	Virtually no risk of spontaneous avalanches.	Routes should be selected with care, especially on steep slopes in the direction and altitude indicated.

136 • *A Complete Guide to Ski Touring and Ski Mountaineering*

3 Considerable	The snowpack is moderate to poorly* bonded on many steep slopes.	Likely to be triggered off even by low additional loads ** on most steep slopes. In some cases, many medium sized and also large spontaneous avalanches expected.	Traffic lines and individual buildings in risk areas at risk in exceptional cases. Precautionary steps should be taken when undertaking safety measures in these areas.	Back country and downhill skiing should only be carried out by experienced people with good avalanche assessment abilities. Steep slopes in the direction and altitudes indicated should be avoided.
4 High	The snow pack is generally poorly bonded and largely unstable.	Numerous large spontaneous avalanches expected, also in moderately steep terrain	This type of avalanche is usually spread over a wide area. Traffic lines and transport facilities in risk areas should occasionally be closed.	No back country and downhill skiing to be undertaken.
5 Very high			Extensive safety measures (closing facilities, evacuation) necessary.	

* Generally described in more detail in the avalanche situation report.
**Additional load; High: group of skiers, piste vehicle, avalanche detonation.
  Low: skier, walker.
Steep slopes are more than 30°.

A Complete Guide to Ski Touring and Ski Mountaineering

8.6 Tactics on the ground

The local avalanche situation is the main factor when deciding where to lay your track or whether to follow the track already there. All other considerations are second place to this.

The observation of the avalanche danger every time you come to a new panorama or different terrain decides:

- To go on or not to go on?
- Where can I lay a safe track?
- Should I implement any extra precautions?

A good track not only keeps you safe from danger but uses the terrain well, moving easily through the line of least resistance. Sometimes the correction of one metre left or right makes all the difference.

Basic points when moving uphill are:

- Tracks already in place are no guarantee of safety and should only be followed when you have made your own assessment of the situation.
- The shortest line is not always the best.
- Do not shy away from safe detours just because it is more hard work. Remember it is the journey to the summit that is important, not the summit itself.
- Avoid long, steep traverses.
- In cornice areas use the safe windward side.
- Use the safer ground on top of spurs and not the slopes on their sides.
- In areas of wind blown snow be sure to avoid the snow deposited areas (gullies, bowls etc).

- Light forest and bushes are not necessarily safe areas. Watch out.

- One group might move forward, the next one turns round and you are standing wondering what to do. Base your decisions on your own knowledge and experience and not on someone else's. If you are unsure turn back and you will have the chance to improve your knowledge and experience for the next tour you go on.

8.6.1 Precautions when skiing uphill

The following basic precautions should be taken into consideration on every tour when moving or skiing uphill:

- Transceiver is always on the body (under a layer of clothing) and switched on to send.

- The transceiver should be checked before every tour to make sure that the batteries are still strong, to make sure that everyone in the group can receive, and to make sure that everyone in the group can send.

- Complete avalanche equipment should be carried, including shovel and probe.

- Known avalanche danger areas avoided.

- The time of the day taken into account (daily rises in temperature, especially in spring, increase the danger).

- Keep a constant eye on changing conditions i.e. terrain, visibility, amount of new snow, temperature and time.

When your observations indicate that the avalanche risk is increasing, then the following extra precautions should be taken to improve the safety of the group:

Spread the group out when moving in avalanche prone terrain.

- Spread the group out to about 10m between each person in order to alleviate the weight on the snow pack. If need be, cross the danger area one at a time.

- Steep slopes of over 30° should be avoided.

- Avoid closing up to other members in the group - keep your distance.

- Remove safety straps from the skis.

- Take your hands out of the ski pole straps.

- Remove the waist belt of the rucksack.

- Put on warm clothing, zip up jackets, and protect breathing area.

- Avoid sudden movements that put extra weight on the snow. A skier resting has his body weight on the snow; moving puts

1-2 times this weight; a kick turn 2-3 times the weight; skiing downhill 3-5 times the weight; and a fall up to 10 times.

Top tips

- These later precautions are used when you are caught out in a situation that you have no control over. If you know that on the tour you will be using them and that the situation is avoidable then the correct decision would be to turn round early and head back down to the valley, staying close to your original track.

In spite of all precautions it is still possible to be caught in an avalanche. It is therefore advisable to put some thought into what you are going to do if this happens.

The following points should be considered:

- If it is possible to go from safe area to safe area then you should cross one at a time with the other team members keeping a look out for any sign of avalanche. If the person crossing is avalanched, then visually mark the spot he was taken from and the spot where he was last seen.

- When moving uphill it is unlikely that an escape route will be much good to you because of your speed of travel.

- Get rid of your ski poles.

- Get your skis off as quick as you can.

- Remove heavy rucksacks.

- Unfortunately it is difficult to prove which movement is best when you are in an avalanche. Reports from survivors say that they tried a swimming action, backstroke, or they tried rolling sideways. An obvious disadvantage of swimming is that the arms, legs and body may end up moving downhill at different speeds resulting in some serious injury, especially in heavy snow.

One thought is to roll together in a ball, arms and legs close to the body, this cuts the injury risk down and at the same time allows you to protect the face and breathing area.

- Just as you feel the snow slowing down try to cover your face and maintain some breathing area. As a final gesture and if you know where the surface is then push an arm towards the surface - your hand might be visible above the snow.

- When the snow has come to a rest try to stay calm and trust in the rest of the group to rescue you.

8.6.2 Precautions when skiing downhill

The same principles of precautions for uphill are used in downhill. As well as that, the following points should be kept in mind:

- Ski in such a way as to put minimum weight on the snow pack. Do not fall, do not hang around. Stick to the line made, and instructions given by the leader. Do not ski swing for swing with a partner thereby putting double the weight on the snow pack. Avoid heavy jumpy turns or slow turns that dig deep into the snow. Keeping your distance away from other skiers helps and this should be 20-30 metres as a minimum.

- If need be, ski one at a time through avalanche danger areas where the avalanche would be channelled.

- In bad visibility, where it is not possible to give a good evaluation of the slope, turn around and head back, staying close to your previous track.

- Compared with moving uphill you have the advantage of speed on your side. A downhill track through avalanche prone slopes should always have escape routes planned in. Generally this would be a straight line out to the left or right to hopefully move off to the side of the avalanche area into a protected or at least safer area.

8.6.3 Considerations if someone is avalanched

As a rule of thumb the chances of survival decrease 50% in the first 30min which means that the first rescue attempts must happen very quickly but without endangering the rescue party. In the early stages after being avalanched most deaths occur either from injuries or from suffocation. After about 90min the only survivors are those with breathing space (without oxygen brain damage begins to occur after about 3-4 minutes). After approximately 2 hours most deaths are caused from a drop in body temperatures. The chances of survival are influenced by a number of things:

- The length of time under the snow.

- The type of snow. Heavy wet snow crushes and has less air.

- The run of the avalanche with a view to obstacles and the likelihood of the avalanched person being thrown against these obstacles.

- The actions of the person being avalanched.

- Not getting rid of skis and ski poles quickly enough. This causes extra twisting levers and more likelihood of injury.

- Not having enough clothing on at the time of the avalanche.

- The speed and efficiency of the rescue party.

How to search

As is probably clear to you by reading the above paragraph, the chances of survival have a lot to do with how quickly and efficiently you implement a rescue. The first hour is often called the golden hour as this is the time when most success is gained and avalanche victims are found alive. The only realistic search at this stage is a transceiver search by the other members of the party and at the same time keeping a good visual look out for any signs of life on the surface. Panic or uncontrolled emotions normally lead to errors in the search. It may be a close friend from your group that you are searching for or an unknown person from another group. You may even feel that you are to blame. Either way a well practiced and systematic search with as cool a head as possible will bring you the best results. Points to consider when searching are:

- Check the area for further danger before charging forward. If possible appoint a look out in the group who stays in a safe area, watching for danger, whistle at hand and also capable of implementing another rescue if you get avalanched.

- Confirm how many people you are searching for.

- If it is another group, confirm that they have transceivers.

- Identify the area where the victim was taken from and the point where the victim was last seen. You will be conducting your search below this point.

- Are there any obvious obstacles where the victim might have been deposited by the avalanche?

- Is there going to be more than one search area?

- How much rescue equipment do you have at your disposal?

- The safety of the people you are responsible for has priority.

- Who is going to organise the search team? A few seconds extra to consider things can save a lot of time rushing around in the wrong direction.

- How capable and experienced are your helpers and how many of them are there?

- Any equipment items sticking out of the snow, after checking them, should be pulled out if possible but left in position for future markings.

- Those not searching should be standing by with shovel and probe to start digging after a searcher has identified the spot.

- If you are searching on your own for several people then anyone you find should have their breathing area cleared and then left there while you search for the others. Some argue that it is better to turn off the transceiver when you find someone - this makes further searching easier - but the negative side of this is that if another avalanche comes down in the mean time the transceiver is not much good. If you are skilful enough to isolate the different tones when searching for several people then leave the transceivers on send for extra safety.

- Check that you are on receive and on maximum distance before you start searching. Remember that mobile phones interfere with transceiver signals.

- Put your spare kit in a depot away from the danger area.

- Do not leave any of your own gear on the avalanche zone as this might confuse later attempts from the mountain rescue teams.

- Think about preparing a helicopter landing area. At least 20m x 20m.

- Sort out first aid kit and possible shelter for any injured people.

- If you have a telephone then the rescue teams should be contacted as soon as it is confirmed that someone is in the avalanche.

- If search dogs are on their way then keep the debris area as clean as possible. Urinating or leaving food scraps only confuses the dogs and prolongs the search.

8.6.4 Digging for the casualty

- Once the digging area has been identified it is important not to cause any damage to the casualty by over enthusiastic digging. Probe a little to get the distance to the casualty. Dig slightly sideways and not directly down. The last few inches to the casualty should be done with hands and not the shovel.

- Identify the head area as quickly as possible and make sure that the breathing area is free.

- Protect the head from any other loose snow falling back onto the casualty.

- If need be administer first aid while others continue digging.

8.6.5 Removing the casualty from the snow

- The body is liable to lose heat faster out of the snow than in it. Make sure you have warm clothing or a sleeping bag ready to put the casualty into.

- Before moving the casualty about it is important to note the extent of the injuries especially the body temperature. Quite often the cause of death is over enthusiastic helpers. It is possible that movement by the casualty can send the cold blood of the extremities to the little bit of warm blood left in the core resulting in the heart giving up.

8.6.6 Organised mountain rescue teams

As soon as it is confirmed that someone is in the avalanche then the mountain rescue should be informed. If you have a telephone then this should be done straight away. If you have no phone or no signal then two experienced members of the party should be sent for help. Before this happens it is important that everyone is used to do an initial search. Remember the statistics - by the time you have a rescue team on the ground the chances of survival for the casualty have decreased considerably.

The two people going for help should have the following:

- Check that their transceivers are back on send.
- The route to the rescue station should be very clearly described.
- What they do after informing the rescue teams should also be made clear.
- They should have a written message containing the following:
  - The location of the accident
  - What happened
  - When it happened
  - How many casualties there are
  - What the condition of the casualties is
  - What the weather and snow conditions are like at the accident spot
  - How many helpers are at the accident spot
  - What equipment the rescuers have got
  - What the experience of the rescuers is and what kind of condition (mentally, physically) they are in

A precise accident report avoids any misunderstanding on the part of the rescuers. While help is being sent for, it is important to continue searching and to make preparations for the rescue team. A helicopter landing area is required and an equipment area far enough away from the landing area. The helicopter landing area needs to be free of obstacles in an area at least 20m x 20m.

Alpine emergency signal

The emergency signal is given as a noise (whistle) or visual (light). 6 times in a minute (one every 10 seconds) with a pause of one minute. The answer is 3 times in a minute (every 20 seconds).

Signal to helicopter pilot

Yes = help required. Both arms held above head in a V shape.

No = no help required or not possible to land. One hand held above head and the other pointing at the ground.

The recognised hand signals to a helicopter

Yes

No

8.7 Search methods

Searching with a transceiver

Searching with the transceiver gives the only realistic chance of finding an avalanche victim. The search technique is generally broken down into three phases:

1. Rough search
2. Fine search
3. Pinpoint search

The transceiver should be held in front of the body and kept facing the same direction as much as possible. The loudness of the receiver tone should constantly be turned down as you approach the victim.

The transceiver should remain attached to the body in case of secondary avalanches.

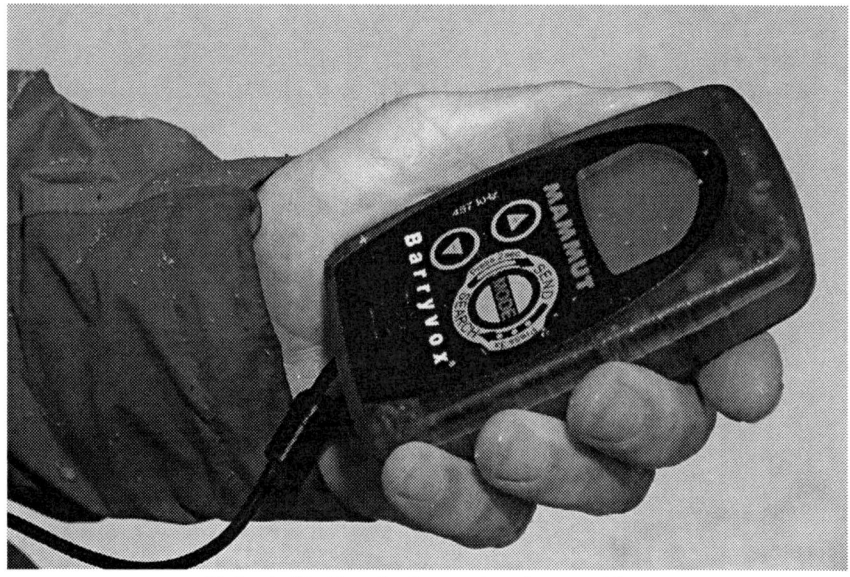

Method of holding the transceiver for searching.

8.7.1 Rough search

Rough search - individual method

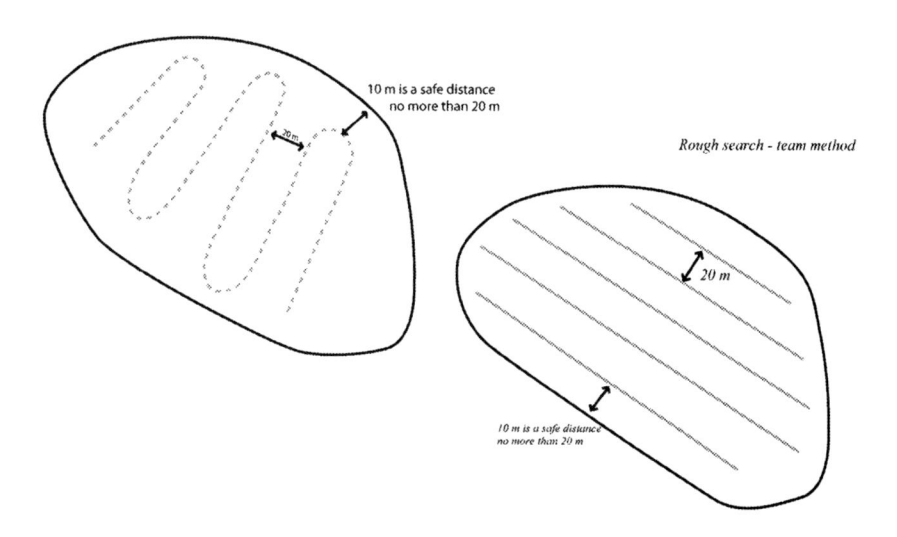

10 m is a safe distance
no more than 20 m

20 m

Rough search - team method

20 m

10 m is a safe distance
no more than 20 m

A Complete Guide to Ski Touring and Ski Mountaineering • 149

When carrying out a rough search there are various measurements recommended by the manufacturers, however these are subject to how strong your batteries are, how good your hearing is, the direction to the buried transceiver and the depth, and by the amount of background noise (as in wind). When using your transceiver it is good to carry out a distance check before you head off on tour and operate any subsequent searches well within your own receiving distance. The style of search can be seen in the following diagram:

- Transceiver search should be started on the highest receiving distance.

- Depending on the width of the avalanche and the number of searchers, the whole area of avalanche debris will be covered by the search and at the same time looking and listening for any other signs of life. The pattern will be either zigzag form (if searching individually) or straight lines (if searching as a team). Start position will be in the likely area of burial. If you are at the top of the avalanche then start at the top and if you are at the bottom then work upwards.

- The search lines must not be further than 20m apart and no further than 10m from the edge of the avalanche.

- As soon as a signal is heard, that point on the ground is marked.

8.7.2 Fine search

Once a signal is heard the fine search system is started. There are two methods for this:

1. Bracketing
2. Flux line

Bracketing

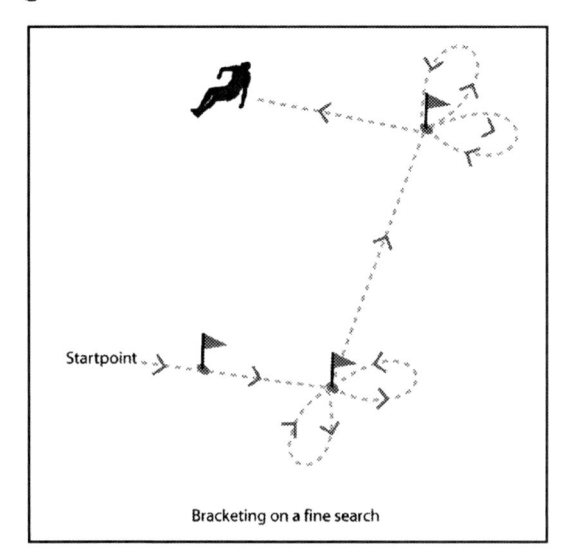

Bracketing on a fine search

- When you pick up the first signal, slowly turn the transceiver until you get the direction with the loudest tone.

- Walk in a straight line in this direction. The tone will get louder and then quieter. Back track on this line until the tone is at its loudest.

- Turn right or left from this line 90°. Walk out on this direction until the tone either gets louder or quieter. Back track until it is at its loudest.

- Change direction again by 90° and repeat the process, each time turning down the volume control until you can still hear it at the 2m volume control.

- When the volume control is at it's lowest and you can still hear a tone you are ready for the pinpoint search.

Flux line

- When you pick up the first signal, slowly turn the transceiver until you get the direction with the loudest tone.

- The direction with the loudest tone is now followed. You are following an oblong shaped line which will take you direct to the casualty. Every few metres stop to recheck the direction of the loudest tone and adjust your forward direction accordingly.

- This is continued each time turning the volume control down until you can still hear the tone when the volume control is at its lowest. You are now ready for the pinpoint search.

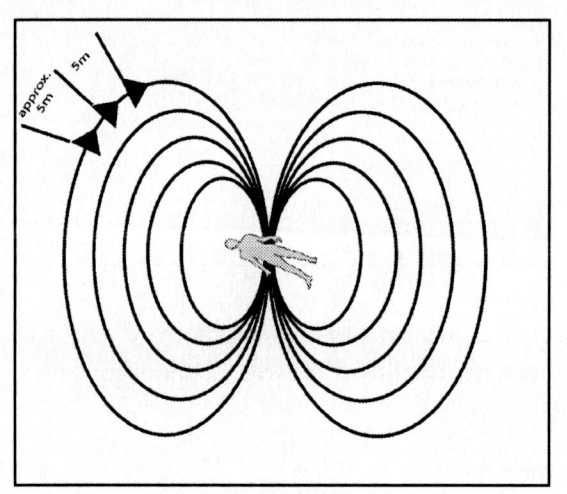

Flux line search.

8.7.3 Pinpoint search

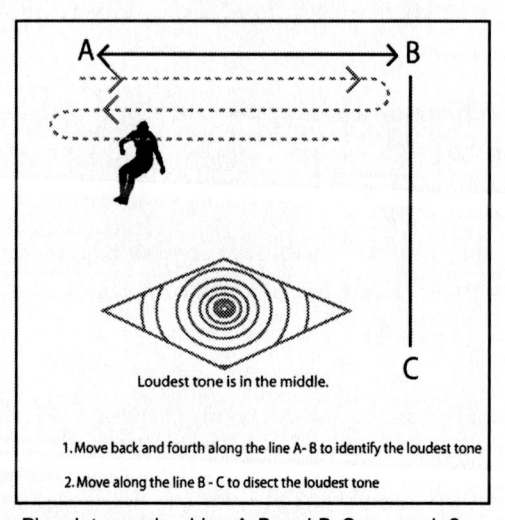

Loudest tone is in the middle.

1. Move back and fourth along the line A-B to identify the loudest tone
2. Move along the line B-C to disect the loudest tone

Pinpoint search. Line A-B and B-C are each 2m.

- For this search you are looking in a square with sides of 2m to pinpoint the exact location. To search here with the transceiver is more a test of transceiver skills as in reality you would also be using a probe to pinpoint the position of the victim.

- The transceiver is held close to the ground and moved slowly back and forth along the square.

- Keep the transceiver facing the same way and you will notice that the outside points of your square are quietest and there is a line down the centre of your square where the tone is loudest.

- Now go to the side of your square and turn the transceiver 90° to your original search. Moving the transceiver along your centre line the loudest tone will put you directly above the victim.

Points to note

- Mobile phones interfere with the signal of transceivers. Keep phones switched off.

- The receiving distance is affected by the strength of the batteries, the direction of the signal and possible obstacles in between you and the victim.

If the search with the transceiver is unsuccessful then the only option open to you is to start probing. There are two probing methods:

1. Course probe
2. Fine probe

Neither probing method is very effective and both normally require a lot of searchers to make them successful. However, if you have been fortunate enough to see the victim moving down the avalanche and have pinpointed the correct area to search in then it can often give very good results.

Course Probe

60 - 75 cm

60 - 75 cm

60 - 75 cm

Fine Probe

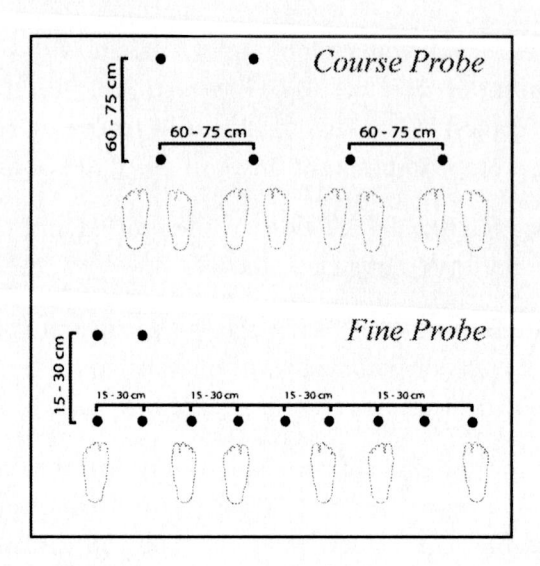

15 - 30 cm

15 - 30 cm 15 - 30 cm 15 - 30 cm 15 - 30 cm

8.7.4 Course probe

- Searchers with transceivers should have them on send.

- The search area is marked with whatever you have available so that you have a better overview of what has been searched and what is still to be searched. It is easier to control if the team are moving uphill.

- The searchers stand shoulder to shoulder in a straight line with the feet a little apart.

- The team controller stands out to the side and endeavours to keep the line straight and the team shoulder to shoulder. The team controller gives the commands 'probes in' and 'forward'.

- The search team insert the probes vertical in the snow, between the feet, to as deep a depth as possible. If nothing is found the probes are removed and the controller then waits until all the probes are out before giving the command 'forward'. If a searcher suspects finding something he should raise an arm and a digging party will take over the digging whilst the searcher moves forward with the rest of the search team and continues searching.

- The probes should be about 60 - 75cm apart and moved forward about the same distance.

- If the probing has to be stopped for any reason the probes are left in the snow to mark the spot to return to.

- The success of probing often depends on the search team doing their job as correctly and conscientiously as possible.

- Ski poles can be used in place of probes if that is all that is available.

8.7.5 Fine probe

- A fine probe is not normally carried out by a ski touring group, more so by mountain rescue teams. It is too time consuming. For the ski touring groups it is more advisable to do a second course probe before starting a fine probe search.

- The formation is the same as for a course probe but the probe is put in the snow in front of the right foot, between the feet, and in front of the left foot with a shorter move forward therefore covering about every 15 – 30cm of ground.

Special note

A fine probe is normally quite successful in finding the victim, but because of the time it takes, whether or not the victim is still alive is questionable. The only realistic avalanche search system is for everyone in the group to have a transceiver and be trained in its use.

9 A Knowledge of Dangers

Various reports on ski touring and ski mountaineering estimate that approximately 70% of accidents are caused by the skiers themselves and that only 10 - 15% of the accident causes are attributed to things outside of the individual's control. It is therefore important to note that, the more participants understand about the dangers involved, the less chance there is of an accident occurring.

Dangers are normally divided into two categories:

- Subjective dangers are those caused by people.
- Objective dangers are those whereby the individual has no control over the occurrence happening but, with careful planning, could do something about avoiding them.

9.1 Subjective dangers

A lack of experience

The correct combination of theory and practice will give you experience. Theory on its own will not suffice nor does it make much sense to head off into the mountains without reading a book similar to this one. To go on a course of instruction under a qualified guide is a very good way of combining both theory and practice. It is also advisable to team up with people who know a little more than you do. Experience and knowledge will increase every time that you go on a ski tour, but it is important that each tour matches your experience at the time.

Everyone's perception of what steep ground is can be different.

A lack of technical ability

Technical ability is achieved by a combination of learning and practice. This book gives you some good tips on how to do the technical skills, what to do and when to do them, but does not confirm to you if you have mastered them. The best thing to confirm that you are doing the skills correctly is to take instruction from qualified people who can make an assessment of your ability (The British Association of Snowsport Instructors for ski skills, Glenmore Lodge or other similar centre offering mountain skills, or a qualified guide or instructor who can match the instruction directly to your requirements).

A lack of physical ability

It is possible, in the Alps, to find some very good quality ski tours under an altitude of 2000m which can be carried out by most people with normal physical ability. On the other hand there are also tours that move between 2000m and 4000m, and any physical activity at these altitudes requires a much greater energy output. It is not everyone's aim to train all year round just to be fit enough to go ski touring. Other commitments also have their priorities, but anyone who is planning to undertake a ski touring trip should match their tour to their physical ability, thereby gaining some enjoyment from the experience. It is also important to the other members of the group that an honest appraisal of your ability is made.

Underestimating the tour

Every tour requires a specific amount of planning, timings estimated, steepness estimated etc., and on tour the correct decisions are made with this planning in mind. No decision should be made under pressure to reach the summit, not to let anyone down, to boost egos, or because the other group have gone forward. Enjoying a day ski touring and safely returning from the mountain has got to be more important to you, your friends, and your family than achieving the aim of the tour but not making it back.

The wrong equipment

There is quite a variety of equipment for ski touring readily available in the shops and, regardless of your budget, it is difficult not to be kitted out with good equipment. It is possible however, perhaps even common, to have the wrong equipment for the job, or to have no equipment for the job at all, or even to have every bit of equipment possible except the one required for the job. Having the best and correct equipment still does not help you if you do not know how to use it, or when to use it. The best answer here is, again, to get some quality instruction from the people qualified to give it. Most equipment today comes with instructions. It is advisable, for a number of reasons, that you read the instructions and practice with it in a safe area before using it on tour.

9.2 Objective dangers

Avalanche

Avalanches are the one danger that the ski tourer is almost constantly faced with. Because of this we have decided to give it its own chapter.

Avalanches are a danger not to be taken lightly.

Crevasse

The main danger for the ski tourer moving over glaciers is that of falling into a crevasse. Avoiding this may come with experience and careful route selection but there are times where there is no alternative but to charge through. In this situation it is a case of roping up and protecting yourself so that any fall does not have serious consequences. Obviously, knowing what to do with the rope in the event of a fall is very important. Crevasses can often be spotted by:

- Slight dips in the snow.

- A change in colour in the snow or light shading.

- A visible change in snow type.

- By looking left and right one can often see larger crevasses and you can then imagine a joined-up line between them.

Weather

The weather with all its differences can be a big problem on a ski tour, and dealing with the weather correctly can be a deciding factor in the enjoyment of the tour. Sun, heat, cold, wet, snowfall, low cloud, wind, storm, and hail all play their part. Along with a good avalanche report, a substantial weather report should be gained before heading out on tour, and during the tour constant weather observations avoid unpleasant surprises.

Sun and heat

Most people new to ski touring in the Alps are surprised by the strength of the sun, and the temperature that can be reached in winter. The bright reflection from the snow adds to this discomfort. Sunburn, heat exhaustion and snow blindness are very common ailments seen on route. When confronted with sun and heat on a ski tour there are some items of equipment that you just do not go without:

Sun and heat might also bring on avalanche prone conditions.

- Quality sunglasses designed for the activity.

- Sun cream with a factor suitable for the job. It is hard to describe exactly which number to choose as everyone's skin is a little different, but I would not choose less than factor 25. If you are coming over direct from the UK then a total sun block might be the answer.

- Lip cream. Most people link sun cream and lip cream (lipsol, lipstick) together but the problems you get and how you get them are different. You should therefore carry a lip stick as standard prevention in, again, a high factor but also some lip cream as treatment for any lip sores. At altitude, if the lips dry out they crack and you are unlikely to sort this out until you get back down to the valley again. This can be very uncomfortable on its own but aggravated when trying to eat and drink. A top tip here is never to share your water bottle with anyone.

- A light sun hat is a must for keeping the sun off your head. Headache, stomach pains and diarrhoea are signs that you have had too much sun.

- Fluids. Here we go…how much should you drink and how much can you carry? In principle drink as much as you can and a little more. Heavy rucksacks when ski touring tend to slow you down and make you sweat more meaning that you require more fluids. Keep your rucksack light and move quickly carrying just enough fluids and a little extra. Get used to drinking at the correct time and rationing your fluids to last the day. I try where possible to take in two litres before moving out in the morning, carry two litres with me, and take in another two litres at least in the evening. Never eat snow to help your fluid intake on a glacier. The bacteria involved is liable to give you more stomach problems than are good for you. Snow should always be boiled before drinking.

Cold and wet

In cold dry air it is fairly straightforward to keep yourself warm with the correct use of clothing. In cold wet conditions (wet snowfall), however, it is another matter. Here the danger of hypothermia comes into play as well as the extra problems of having your kit freeze over, making it very difficult sometimes to get it in and out of your rucksack. The correct clothing and the correct amount of it are very important and the ability to keep moving at a pace to generate enough heat. Frost nip or even frost bite are also a problem and not just on exposed skin. Keep an eye on your own extremities, and those of your partner, from time to time checking for white spots (cheeks, nose, ear lobes and fingers are the easy parts to check). When the fingers stop working you are beginning to lose control of the situation so it is important to have enough pairs of gloves to hand.

After a recent snow fall rocks like these are often very difficult to see from above.

Snow fall and low cloud

Snow fall and low cloud often bring with it white-out conditions (where it is impossible to identify the horizon) but always bring poor visibility or flat light conditions. This on its own is often a good reason to break off the tour. These sort of conditions make it very difficult to navigate, but more importantly make it almost impossible to identify avalanche prone slopes. It is important to know whether conditions are going to get better (in which case you might be able to sit it out) or worse (in which case the sooner you make the decision to get off the hill the better).

Poor visibility makes navigation very difficult, and identifying any dangers almost impossible.

Wind and storm

Coming from the UK where a bit of wind is the norm, it can be quite easy to underestimate wind and storms in the Alps. The wind takes heat away from the body at a rapid rate (especially if clothing is wet), it drops the air temperature, it freezes wet clothing and equipment, and brings on cold injuries very quickly. If the storm does not let up then it is very difficult to reverse this heat loss process. As well as this the communication within the group is considerably more difficult. When skiing downhill in a storm, especially with bad visibility, it is very difficult to judge your movement and speed of descent as well as keeping the group together. In these situations it is much better to have everyone ski in the same track.

This may look pretty, but high winds are an indication that other dangers are lurking.

Hail

Not as common in the Alps in winter as it is in the summer, nevertheless it is a definite problem as it comes with lightning strikes. At these times you most definitely do not want to be anywhere near ridges or summits, or fixed wires (Klettersteigs) that are sometimes part of a tour. Approaching storms with hail and lightning are fairly easy to predict because of the typical build-up of clouds.

Rockfall

Rockfall is obviously only a danger if your tour takes you into rocky terrain. It is normally caused by the water freezing in the rocky cracks which splits the rock further but holds it in place until such time as the sun comes out and melts the ice holding the rock. This loose rock often stays in place until such times as a group walk over it on their way to a summit. Watch your footing, be careful not to knock anything off onto people below you, and be watchful of groups above you.

Icefall

This is generally a glacier problem where there are hanging glaciers over your route, or seracs that you have to go through. The problem with icefall is that it is not dependant on the time of day, and unlike avalanches, is very difficult to predict. The problem here is that the glacier is quite simply sliding very slowly downhill, eventually the weight of anything hanging over an edge becomes too heavy to support, and falls off. Take local advice on any recent glacier movement, do not hang around when moving through serac areas and on no account stop for a rest under hanging glaciers.

Cornices

Deciding along which line a cornice is liable to crack requires a little bit of experience. In addition to this you need knowledge of where the ridge line is and how much snow has formed up. If in doubt give yourself a good allowance for error and stay well over on the safe side. Cornices that build up only in the winter are a lot less stable than the more permanent cornices that you might find in summer or winter in areas over 3000m.

Altitude

Altitude is one of the problems that could reasonably fit into both categories of danger. On most tours it will not be a problem, but one should remember that some of Europe's mountains are over 4000m in height and a lot of them can be reached fairly easily on skis. Most medical books will give you detailed signs and symptoms of illnesses and ailments to do with altitude, along with their treatments and preventions. Here are a couple of points worth noting: up to about 2000m is generally not a problem, above this height it is worth thinking of a little bit of acclimatisation, especially if you are coming direct from the UK. If your tours are going to take you over 3000m then it is advisable to read up on altitude sickness before you go.

Nightfall and emergency shelter

During the main winter months the days are shorter and darkness often catches up with you very quickly. Think about planning shorter tours, and possibly giving yourself a couple of hours buffer zone at the end of the tour or even setting out a little earlier (the infamous alpine start). You never know what sort of problems could arise to slow you down: heavy snow, damaged equipment, illness or injury en route. A good head torch might see you to the end with little problem, and if the worst comes to the worst then having the necessary equipment with you to dig out an emergency shelter should see you through the night without any major problems.

10 The Weather

A successful ski tour is essentially when the group reach their summit, enjoy a great ski down and feel that they have not been exposed to any great avalanche danger on the way. This success and enjoyment is largely dependent on the weather. With ideal touring weather, the ski tour group can relish the summits (obviously still observing the local avalanche danger) without having to worry about finding the way back to the hut through fogs and snow drifts. However, if a change in the weather and consequently a change in the snow pack are expected or if one is caught by surprise with a sudden weather change, some knowledge of the weather is necessary Experience will come to those who spend a lot of time in the mountains and this experience can help determine when the weather is going to change. This is important when selecting routes which have avalanche prone slopes incorporated within them.

The judgment of the long-term weather should be a basic component of the tour plan in order to get in front of immediate dangers (fog, cold, etc) and out of indirect dangers from the weather (wet, freeze). Observing meteorological reports will ensure you will not be caught out. An overnight stop in a hostile environment is not a good experience.

Top tip:
- The weather influences the conditions on the way up, the snow texture for the ski down and also the avalanche danger. Experience, knowledge and understanding of the weather contributes to the success and security of every ski tour.

A good day for touring

10.1 Basic knowledge

As well as understanding weather reports from different sources it is important to understand where the weather comes from. Three main factors effecting weather are air temperature, atmospheric pressure and humidity.

Climatic differences are caused in the first instance by the differing amounts of solar radiation received on different parts of the Earth's surface. Polar, Ferrell & Hadley cells are warmed up by the sun. They influence the weather depending on where they lie around the world.

Air pressure is air in motion and is measured in millibars - a high pressure system is that which lies above 1013 millibars and moves in a clockwise direction. A low pressure system is that which lies below 1013 millibars and moves in an anticlockwise direction.

Millibars are the standard measurement for air pressure.

We are affected by 4 different weather systems or air streams and each of these weather systems has a typical weather pattern:

* Polar maritime   -   wet and cold
* Polar continental   -   cold and dry
* Tropical, continental -   warm and dry
* Tropical maritime   -   Warm but moist

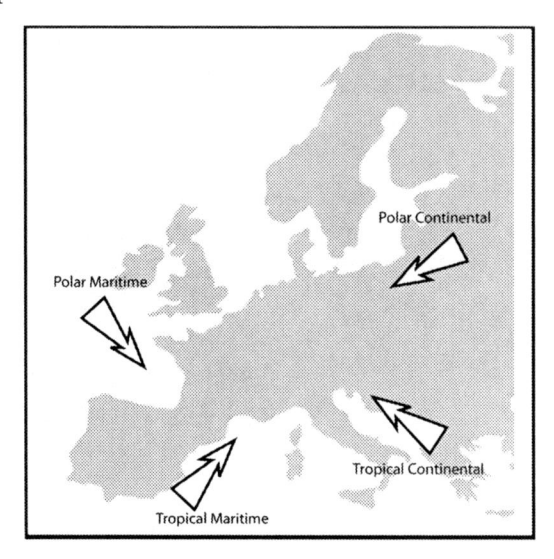

Where to obtain weather reports

There are a number of areas where it is possible to obtain a weather report that would be suitable for ski touring. The best options are obviously the local forecasts for the area that you are in and not a national forecast giving you a general report for the whole country. With a little searching around you will soon find out for yourself which reports are the most reliable.

* TV
* Radio
* Newspaper

- * Telephone
- * Fax
- * Internet
- * Local Knowledge (lift companies normally have a weather report posted within the cable car station)
- * Folk lore

10.2 Vertical climate structure

The highest point of the Alps (4807m) is Mont Blanc in France, closely followed by the Dufourspitze (4634m). Only 48 km east of this lies a large lake at 193m. A relative height difference of 4441m results from it. This clarifies the weather difference between the two, because weather elements as you rise in altitude change.

10.2.1 Effects with increasing height

- The atmospheric pressure and the humidity decrease continually.
- The oxygen sinks to 61% (of that at sea level) at 4000m high.
- Temperature drops (Lapse rate) by up to 1° of temperature per 100m when the air is clear and dry & 1° per 200m when the air is cloudy and wet.
- The radiation from the sun rises (UV-radiation)

10.2.2 Cloud formation

Through the sun's radiation, water evaporates. This rises as steam. If the saturation point (dew point) is reached (the air with 100 % of steam is enriched), the condensation process begins. The steam becomes microscopically small particles and then water-droplets, and then the clouds become visible.

One distinguishes clouds by the layers that appear at different heights. On the basis of this shape, the ski tourer can watch the developments on regional weather and make correct judgements.

10.2.3 Precipitation

From a certain height, the moisture drops and is recorded as precipitation. This precipitation can fall as rain or in frozen form as snow, sleet or hail. Hail droplets are little water drops, that are carried in the cold zone of the cloud by up-currents which freeze the water drops immediately. Condensation is the steam at ground level on a cold surface (one speaks of dew). Rime develops if the moisture is frozen solidly without passing through the gas stage (sublimation). This is an appealing sight, however the danger is instantly recognisable (wind direction of new snow being deposited).

10.2.4 Observing the clouds

The experienced ski tourer can observe the cloud formations and recognise the signs of approaching weather danger (storms, cold, or precipitation). In order to recognise a forthcoming weather front, one must understand how fronts work and build. Once this lesson is learnt, judgements can be made before, during, and at the later stages of the tour. For example, a sequence of a typical cold front approaching would show: stratus in middle layers, precipitation clouds in low layers, cumulus in all layers.

cold and warm fronts showing the cloud and rain types

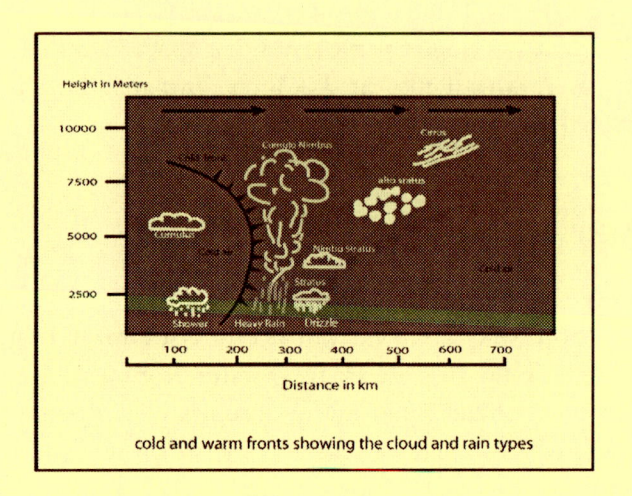

Cirrus

Cirrus clouds are the highest in the Atmosphere (8000-12000m) and can move very fast (approximately 100km/h). They consist of ice crystals and have a white, silky look. Cirrus clouds are signs of weather change if they build from the South West and move North West. Cirrus clouds from the East are signs of good weather to come.

Cirrus clouds

Cirrostratus

If Cirrus builds, it can form a type of veil, which sometimes covers the complete sky. The sun can shine through them and therefore forms a typical sun ring (halo). Cirrostratus are signs of precipitation. The atmospheric pressure drops indicating bad weather to come.

Cirrocumulus

The Cirrocumulus belongs to the group of the high clouds. They move in a height of 6000 - 10000m. Cirrocumulus clouds are a sign of approaching thunderstorms.

Altocumulus

This classic little cloud can be found at a height between 3000m - 6000m. It is a white and grey, middle sky cloud. When these clouds appear in a tower-style bad weather follows. You can calculate that thunderstorms will follow with possible snow & sleet depending on the time of year. If the clouds are flatter in shape then good weather follows.

Stratocumulus

These clouds appear frequently between 500 - 2000m. They build in bale formations and their appearance is typical in a morning sky.

High clouds clearly separated from the cumulus build up below the sun.

Cumulus

These are thick, isolated clouds, which either dissolve, or build up into towers through the course of the day.

Cumulus clouds

Cumulonimbus

Cumulonimbus are very high cloud formations which look like a cauliflower or an anvil. These clouds mean that thunderstorms with precipitation and hail are imminent.

10.3 Observation of the wind

The appearance of the weather and wind plays an important part in any judgement made by experienced ski tourers. Every ski tourer knows the cooling effect of a light wind in the afternoon on a hot ski tour, or the cooling unpleasant glacial wind on an early start that presses cold clothes onto the body, or the strength of a strong wind that hinders forward momentum. These wind types are the series of air movements that originate through regional atmospheric pressure and temperature differences which move with different speeds. An important point for the ski tourer, is to be able to recognize and interpret the wind strength and wind direction. The wind strength is measured in km/h and in a 10-step scale known as the Beaufort scale (see below).

BEAUFORT SCALE	KMPH	DESCRIPTION	EFFECTS ON A SKIER	HOW COLD IS +5°C?
1 – 3	2 - 20	Light air, light breeze, gentle breeze	Good skiing day, but snow could be moving around.	3 to -2
4	21 – 29	Moderate breeze	Wind chill cools you fast on the summits.	-6
5	30 – 39	Fresh breeze	Extra care needed on ridges and scrambles.	-8
6	40 – 50	Strong breeze	The snow is now horizontal. Forward movement on skis is difficult. Avoid ridges.	-9
7	51 – 61	Near gale	Ski lifts probably not open.	-12
8	62 – 74	Gale	Ropes blow horizontally.	-14
9	75 – 87	Strong gale		-18
10	88 - 100	Storm		-20

Beaufort wind scale showing wind speed, effects on skiers and the temperature with the wind chill factor.

The wind direction can be determined with the use of a compass. The direction in which the clouds are moving, snow cornices, and when loose snow is deposited in a certain direction, or even a cloth held into the wind all show the original direction of the wind.

Top tip:
- Wind is the master builder of wind slab avalanches. It is responsible for transporting snow from one area to another, from the windward side to the lee side (as described early in the avalanche chapter). Above all, it deposits large amounts of snow into gullies and bowls.

10.3.1 Wind movements

Air movements either happen in a vertical or a horizontal direction. As the horizontal winds develop, the air masses try to equalize between high and low pressures. For the ski tourer this means strong or weak winds, in areas of very different atmospheric pressure. At the weather fronts one can expect extreme weather conditions and strong winds and this should indicate to the tourer to avoid lee areas, bowls and gullies.

10.3.2 General wind types

Within the mountains, with their steep-sided valleys and high summits, the wind can change considerably from one end of the valley to the other. This is caused mainly by the changes in daily temperatures. A common wind type found here is that of mountain and valley winds (katabatic, anabatic).

A fohn wind is a classic wind in the northern Alps. It starts as a moist wind from the south and as it climbs up over the Alps this moisture is lost in precipitation. On it's way down the north side of the Alps it is characterised as a very warm dry wind. The clouds seem to hang like a wall in a straight line over the east – west line of the summits, and the north side has clear sunny days. This warm air flow has the disadvantage that it eats the snow up and can sometimes be strong enough to close the lift systems.

The reason why a fohn happens

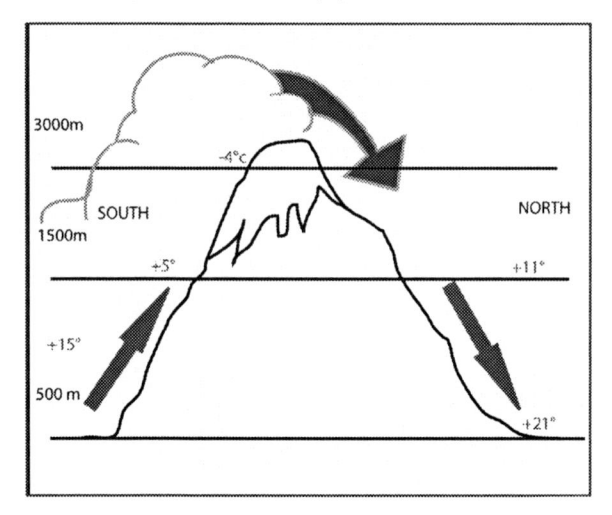

In the diagram above, the air is rising on the south side of the mountain and is cooling down at 0.6°C for every 100m of height gain whilst in cloudy and moist air, once passing over the summit, the air warms up at 1°C every 100m of height lost thus being able to hold more moisture and allowing better weather on the north side.

Observations

- Fohn winds are very common in Alpine resorts. Be aware that the air on the north side will be very warm, increasing avalanche danger and developing a very unstable snow pack.

- As the wind is pulled over the summit, cigar shape clouds will form at different heights.

- Local folk say when a Fohn is present the weather will not stabilise for an odd number of days i.e. if the Fohn starts on day one it will stop on day 3 or 5 or 7 but not on day 2 or 4.

10.3.3 Local winds of the Alps

Mountains can cause local winds to become stronger on windward sides and less strong on lee sides of mountains. A saddle is always the wrong place to hang around as the winds are stronger there than on the sides of the mountain. Be aware that winds on the mountain summits and ridges will increase, thus increasing wind chill and avalanche danger on lee sides.

Top tips:

- Wind strength can hinder the ski tour - when the wind is about 37 km/h it will be hard to progress and ridges and summits should be avoided.

- The chill at about 37 km/h is approximately -5° not taking into account the height and the texture of the wind (dry or damp).

- The wind can, in a few hours, increase the avalanche risk considerably. The snow will be moved around with a wind speed of 30 km/h.

- Wind will cover the tracks you have made, so be sure you have correct navigation equipment with you.

- Ensure you stand with your back to the wind and for longer rests find a good wind-sheltered place.

10.4 Further weather observation

As well as making note of the official Alpine weather report and observation of clouds and wind to make your own forecast, there are other factors that you can use to make your predictions more accurate. These are atmospheric pressure, temperature and humidity and they can be checked at virtually every mountain hut within the Alps as most of them have a small weather station.

10.4.1 Atmospheric pressure

The atmospheric pressure varies with altitude. At sea level the air pressure has an average value 1013mb - this pressure is measured with a barometer. With every 10m climbed, the atmospheric pressure decreases by 1mb, so that by the time you are at 6000m it is approximately half of its sea level value. The temperature has an effect on the atmospheric pressure - cold air is heavy and sinks while warm air extends and rises. Don't forget, as you increase height the temperature decreases by approximately 1°c per 100m.

If you are carrying an altimeter with you (which you should be) then this can be used as a barometer when you overnight in the hut.

Important points

- A slow pressure drop - prolonged bad weather is expected.
- A fast pressure change - very unsettled weather can be expected.

Top tips:

- Weather changes at the same time as the air pressure changes - observe barometers.
- Fast atmospheric pressure drops means storms. Fast atmospheric pressure rises mean only a short clearing.
- Pressure drops of 5mb are normal within the day. This drop of pressure is a consequence of the air warming.
- 1mb decrease corresponds to 10m of height.

10.4.2 Air temperature

The air temperature drops with the increase of height (lapse rate). The air temperature drops 1° every 100m in dry still air but 1° every 200m in cold damp air.

A Complete Guide to Ski Touring and Ski Mountaineering

Temperature also varies when frontal systems are approaching. Before a warm front there will be a slow rise. Before a cold front there will be a sudden fall in the temperature.

Top tips:

- Zero degrees centigrade is the normal temperature point where snow can fall, however snow can fall at +1.5°C.

- The temperature will vary as you move around, therefore if you are using the temperature as a gauge for weather prediction it will be more accurate if you always take it in the same spot and, to be more precise, the same time each day.

10.4.3 Humidity

Air consists of water in gas form. The steam quantity existing within one cubic meter of air is absolute humidity. Humidity is expressed in %. Warm air can hold more moisture than cold air so if the temperature continues to sink then at some stage 100% of relative humidity will be reached, droplets form and precipitation occurs.

As you become more experienced in the mountains your knowledge of the weather will increase.

11 Some Rescue and Emergency Techniques

With a few extra skills it is possible to look after yourself and your team when the requirement of a rescue exists. In this chapter we are going to concentrate on crevasse rescue and overnighting in snow shelters. The causes, or the results, of these incidents may well require you to administer first aid or some other medical treatment. Each individual going into the mountains in summer or winter should ensure that they have some kind of first aid training and a basic understanding of aches, pains, cuts, bruises, blisters and bleeding. It is not in the scope of this book to go into the subject of first aid or medicine, and if you require such training then there are any number of good books on the market as well as official organisations offering training. Some addresses are given in chapter 15.

11.1 Crevasse rescue

In spite of good route selection, it is sometimes impossible to avoid crevasse areas and when this is the case it is also not so easy to ensure that someone in the team will not drop into one. If this happens then it is important for all of the team, including the person in the crevasse, to keep calm but work quickly in order to ensure a successful return to normal. By each method of rescue it is normal for the person in the crevasse, when possible, to take the skis off and hang them under the body attached to a sling or end of the rope, thereby keeping them out of the way.

Crevasse rescue is best practiced in a safe area before going on tour.

11.1.1 Self rescue

A self rescue can be used when the person in the crevasse is not injured and the rest of the rope team are not capable of implementing a rescue.

- **Prusik technique**. For this method a long and a short prusik loop are attached to the main rope. The shorter of the two should be on the top and attached to the harness. The long prusik is used for a foot loop, and when the knee is at full bend should reach to the top one. Variations of this are possible and it is important to play around with the lengths until you get what is comfortable for you. If you are using a full harness where the attaching point to the harness is higher, it is possible to have the long leg loop above the shorter one.

- **Alpine clutch method.** When the rope has cut into the snow bridge it is often difficult to get the prusiks over the top. It might be easier to use an alpine clutch. The start method is the same as for the prusik system. Once you have enough rope (usually 1.5m) an alpine clutch is put into the sit harness using this spare rope. A karabiner is attached to a small prusik higher up the main rope. The spare rope from the alpine clutch is now put through this karabiner and you have yourself a little pulley system. The technique here is to lift the hips high with the feet against the crevasse and heave yourself on the pulley system. Then rest on the clutch and move the prusik further up the main rope.

A Complete Guide to Ski Touring and Ski Mountaineering

11.1.2 Team rescues

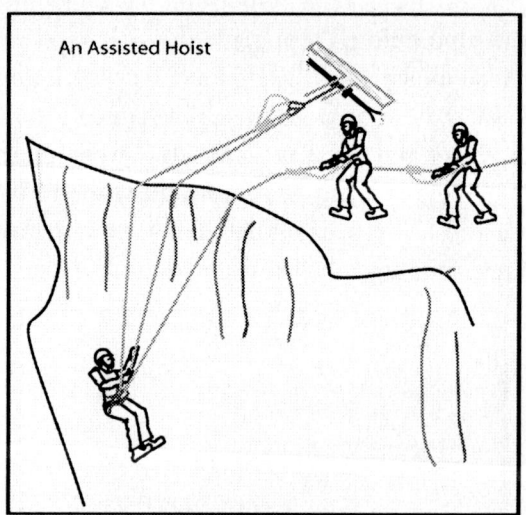

An Unassisted Hoist

An Assisted Hoist

Team rescues are the norm on glaciers and the method you use depends on the amount of people in a team. Large teams might be able to just walk backwards and pull the casualty out of the crevasse. Smaller teams will more than likely have to use one of the following pulley systems. Both methods start with the team going to ground and bringing the skis across the direction of travel in order to hold the fall. The number two and three communicate with one another and the number three holds the weight whilst the number two sets up a suitable belay. A French prusik is used to attach the number one rope (the rope leading to the casualty) to the anchor point and the weight lowered off the number three and onto this prusik. The loose rope is now put into a belay device and also attached to the belay by the number two. The number three now moves forward, protecting himself as he goes with a short prusik, after this the two following methods separate.

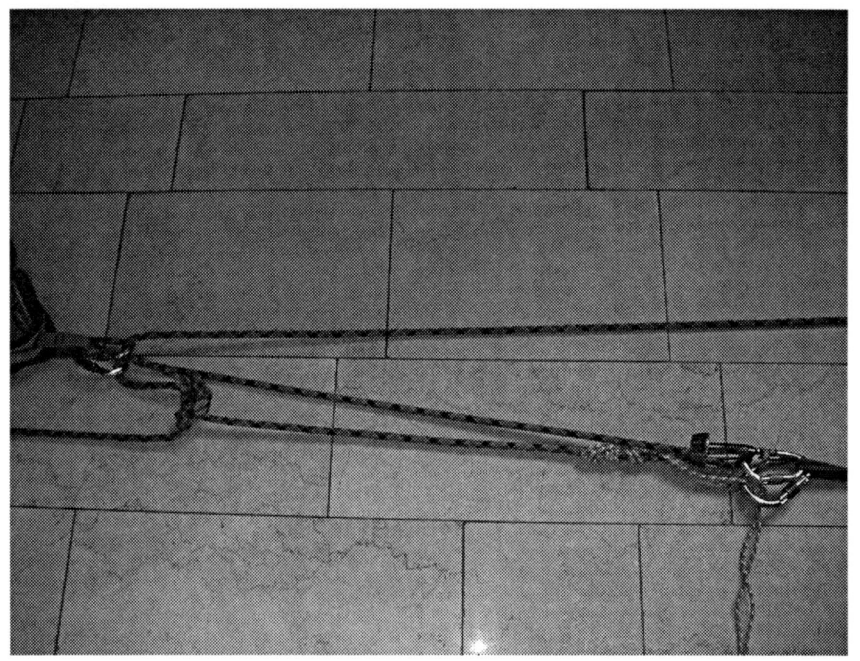

A pulley system for an assisted hoist.

- **Assisted hoist.** An assisted hoist can be used when the casualty is capable of helping. The number two rope (the one coming out of the other end of the belay device from the number one rope) is now passed down to the casualty who clips it into the harness. The number three has kept hold of his end of the rope and you now have a zig zag of rope, attached at one end to the number one, running through the belay device, back down to the number one, back again to the number three. To operate the hoist, the number one pulls on the 2nd rope and the number three pulls on his end of the rope. The number two keeps an eye on the belay.

- **Unassisted hoist.** When the casualty is not capable of helping, or if the team is capable of operating the hoist on their own, the unassisted hoist is used. Instead of passing the rope down to the casualty, put a short prusik on the number one rope as close to the edge as you can, clip a karabiner into it and clip the number two rope into this karabiner (3:1 hoist). The number two and three now pull together on the number three rope.

A pulley system for an unassisted hoist.

With the above descriptions it is indeed possible to work out the theoretical principles, but it is also possible to make some serious errors in the routine or the type of safety. It is, therefore, preferable that these rescues should be practiced under the supervision of a qualified person before going on tour.

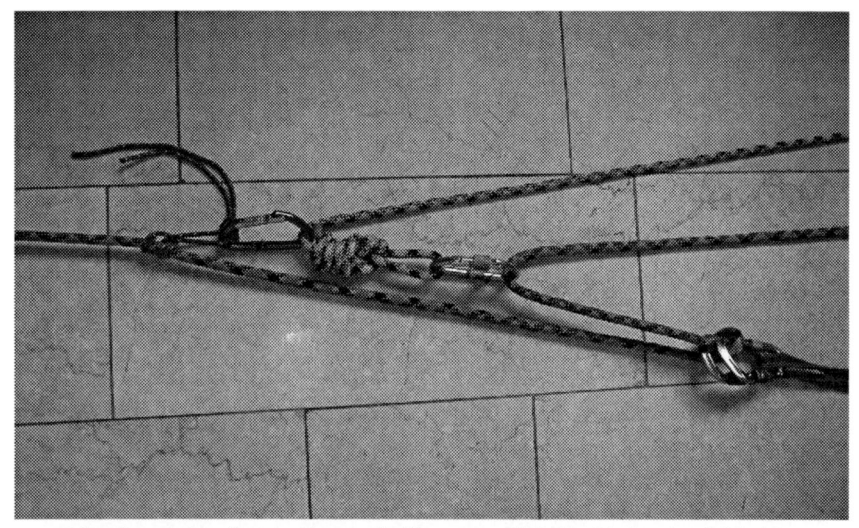

A pulley system that can be used with an unassisted hoist showing 5:1 hoist.

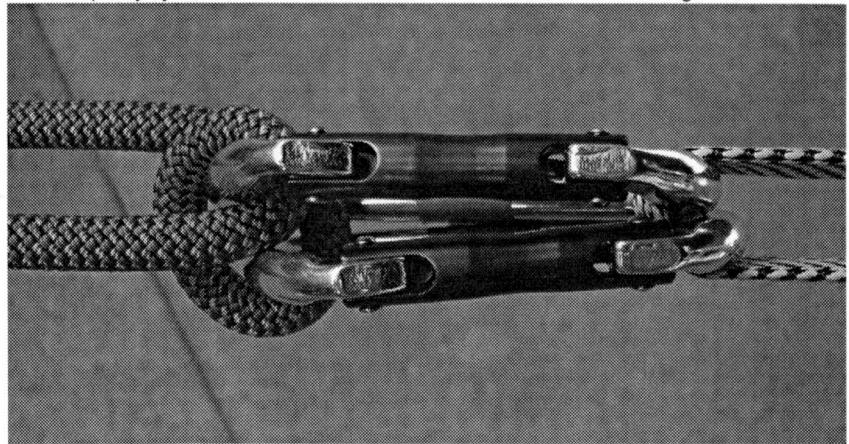

An alpine clutch can be used instead of a belay device and French prusik.

11.2 First aid and accident procedure

After a fall or accident with an injury, by an avalanche for example, it is necessary that the group are capable of delivering some basic first aid or medical treatment at the scene. In bad weather it can often be some time until the rescue services get to you and for this reason having a telephone is a must. Because of this possible delay it is important that a good routine is stuck to until help is available. If the injuries from the casualty are such that it is not possible for him to help himself along to the next hut then the following routine should be carried out:

- Assess the accident situation.

- Look for dangers and keep yourself and the rest of your team safe.

- Protect the casualty from further danger, and if need be move him to a safe area.

- Check for life threatening conditions - airway, breathing, circulation, bleeding - and prevent the condition from getting any worse.

- Check for injuries, breaks, shock, drop in body temperatures, and treat accordingly. Watch out for the not so obvious.

- Keep the casualty as comfortable and warm as possible.

- Consider how to transport the casualty to safety.

- During the whole process keep an eye on everyone else in the group as someone else might be affected by the whole thing and also suffering from shock.

The main three dangers when digging someone out of an avalanche are:

- Suffocation

- Injury, breaks, cuts, head wounds

- General drop in body temperature (hypothermia)

11.3 Snow shelters

There are times when things do not go quite as planned. An injury in the group, a broken ski, a navigation error, being surprised how quickly darkness sets in - all of which make it impossible or too dangerous to carry on to the hut. In such cases you might be left with no alternative but to overnight in the snow. No panic, with a slick routine, a few tips, and a bit of practice, the evening can be quite comfortable and actually good fun. The first thing to note is that the temperature drops quickly at night and if accompanied by wind can be quite life threatening. The best way to counter this is to get active, start digging at a pace to keep yourself warm but not to exhaust you. As soon as you have a wind break erected you will find it much more comfortable, and once you have dug in a little you will realise that the temperature is getting quite warm. Be careful here because when you stop digging the temperature drops even faster. You should, with a little practice, be able to dig a shelter for yourself within 1.5 - 2 hours, depending on the snow hardness. The following explains to you the equipment that you need and how to go about digging a shelter.

Make sure that you have enough depth down the way as well as in.

Equipment

- Essential items are: shovel, probe, bivy bag, head torch, spare gloves and possibly a snow saw.

- Extra items for comfort are: dry spare clothes, a candle and matches, cooker, warm hand pads, sleeping bag, flask, drink and food stuff, small mat to lie or sit on.

Where and how to dig

- The area must be free from any danger (avalanche, ice fall, rock fall, crevasse).

- The best areas are steep snow banks where you can dig in standing upright. It is also possible if you are on the flat to dig down into a trench if there is enough snow, and if there is not enough snow to build up in an igloo type structure.

- Where possible keep the entrance away from the wind.

- Use your probe to check for depth both down the way (vertical depth) and inwards (horizontal depth).

- Pace yourself when digging and think about eating and drinking as you progress - it can be hard work.

- There are various methods to dig but I prefer to dig a narrow doorway straight in at head height for about six feet.

- I then turn left or right and hollow out a sleeping platform that I can sit on without my head touching the roof. The initial trench acts as a cold air well (cold air sinks so make sure you are not lying at the bottom of your snow hole).

- Smooth out the roof and slope it a little to the edges so that any water or moisture runs to the edges and does not drip onto the sleeping area.

- Block up the large entrance and then dig a small hole to crawl in through, which in turn can be blocked from the inside with rucksacks.

- Make sure you have an air hole somewhere.

- If you have time you can now start thinking about the luxury things - digging small compartments for your gear and extra areas to move around in.

Routine in the snow hole

Regardless of the type of snow shelter it is very important to have a routine. There are two main reasons for this:

Inside a snow shelter.

1. To make life comfortable for yourself and anyone else that you are sharing with.

2. To ensure that if things get worse (snow hole collapses, lights go out) you have everything organised and under control, basically,

to ensure that you all have a safe night. All the measures that you take should be designed to keep yourself warm but avoid exhaustion. Moving and doing something also makes the time pass better and has a better psychological feeling than sitting and waiting. The following list will help you on your way:

- If it is an emergency shelter then you are unlikely to have a lot of gear with you. Use something to insulate between yourself and the snow (a rope, a rucksack, any bushes you may have seen nearby). Get some dry clothes on next to the skin and then whatever other clothes you have. Cuddle up close to someone to improve heat and every now and then move around to keep yourself warm.

- Mark the outside of the snow hole with crossed skis above (this ensures that no one skis in through your roof) and also mark the entrance with possibly a spare probe. If there is more than one shelter think about where the other entrances are in case you have to go and help the others dig out. Possibly connect the entrances with a rope.

- Keep a shovel inside the snow hole.

- Throughout the night keep a check on the airway.

- Keep your transceiver on in case someone else needs to find you.

- If the extremities start feeling cold do something about it early and, if possible, get your partner to help. This also gives your partner a sense of purpose.

- If you are cooking then keep all the stoves away from your kit (you will not want to spill anything over your sleeping bag). Consider the fumes given off by the various stoves. Make a separate alcove, where possible, for cooking. Think about the possibility of a fire, leaking fuel, someone changing a gas canister, and how you can get out. It is better, if conditions allow, to cook outside and if this is not possible then think about a separate entrance to the snow hole for a cooking area.

- Anything damp or with moisture in it is likely to freeze before the morning. Gloves will be solid, water bottles frozen and if there is some water in the thread of the screw top of the bottle then you will probably not be able to open the bottle. Put anything you do not want to freeze into a plastic bag and take it into your sleeping bag with you. In the morning it will still be wet, but warm.

- In winter I normally carry a couple of warm pads with me. There are various types in the shops. The ones I use, after breaking the seal, will stay warm for about 12 hours and I just put them between the two pairs of socks that I am wearing in my sleeping bag and that is my feet sorted out for the night. If you warm up some water just before getting into your bag, depending on the type of bottle you have, you can shove it under your shirt which works like an old fashioned hot water bottle keeping the core temperature nice and cosy.

- Skis and ski poles, group shelters, bivy bags, and skins can all be used to help out with roof construction. The larger items, like skis, are placed across the top. The smaller items are used to make a mesh-work pattern. The bivy bags are placed on top of this and then the whole thing can be covered over with snow.

12 Planning A Tour

Many accidents that happen when ski touring can be traced back to basic mistakes in the planning stages. Much has to be taken into consideration when planning and these points are laid out below. Careful planning will add a lot to the enjoyment and safety of the tour, and is just as important as being able to move quickly, to ski well, or to be in good physical condition.

Careful planning of the tour is an essential part of the preparations.

Touring area

- Where to tour, the correct maps, guide books, how to get there, lifts, language, rescue cover, medical treatment, currency.

- Hut system - guardian or no guardian, winter room, opening dates, services available.

- Other facilities in the area, overnight possibilities in valley, alpine information - weather/avalanche reports, supermarkets, banks, restaurants.

General snow and avalanche situation

- Snow conditions at various altitudes and aspects.
- Avalanche report with a history of the previous week and a forecast for whether the danger will increase or decrease over the next few days.
- Which areas are more dangerous than others or are specifically prone to avalanche, slope steepness, aspect or altitude.
- Any good reliable local knowledge to do with the avalanche situation.

Weather situation

- An up-to-date weather report with a history of what has been happening and a forecast of what is expected to happen.
- Wind influence, sunshine influence, temperature variations, precipitation developments.

Time of year

- Sunrise and sunset timings.
- Ensure that the selected ski touring area suits the time of year.

Physical and technical ability of the group

- How strenuous is the tour?
- How technical and difficult is the way up?

- What skiing standard is needed for the way down?

Choice of route

- General avalanche danger for both up and down.
- Avalanche danger on specific slopes both up and down.
- Any alternative routes to avoid danger.

Technical difficulty of the route and mountaineering requirement

- Height difference up and down.
- Any technical passages of climbing, ice, rock or a combination of them.
- Other difficulties because of the altitude, the weather or the present conditions.
- The overall requirement of the route.

Time available

- An approximate time for up and down. This may vary considerably due to conditions on the ground or the ability and condition of the group.
- Calculate into your estimations: time required for rests, photo stops and equipment problems.
- Plan to finish your tour with enough daylight hours in reserve for any emergencies that might occur.

Equipment

- It almost goes without saying - make sure you have the correct equipment necessary for the job and that you know how to use it.

- Consider the time of year and the possible weather and temperature fluctuations.

- Decide what is going to be the group equipment and what is required as individual equipment.

- Check all your equipment before setting out. Check that it works, how it works, that it is functional, that it is necessary (weight), and decide what you need to take as spares or repair kit.

Information sources

- Maps, preferably 1:25000

- Guide books

- Guides office, tourist office or hut guardian

- Weather and avalanche report (internet is a very good source)

- Information from people who have been in the area before

- Information from official organisations (see chapter 15—addresses)

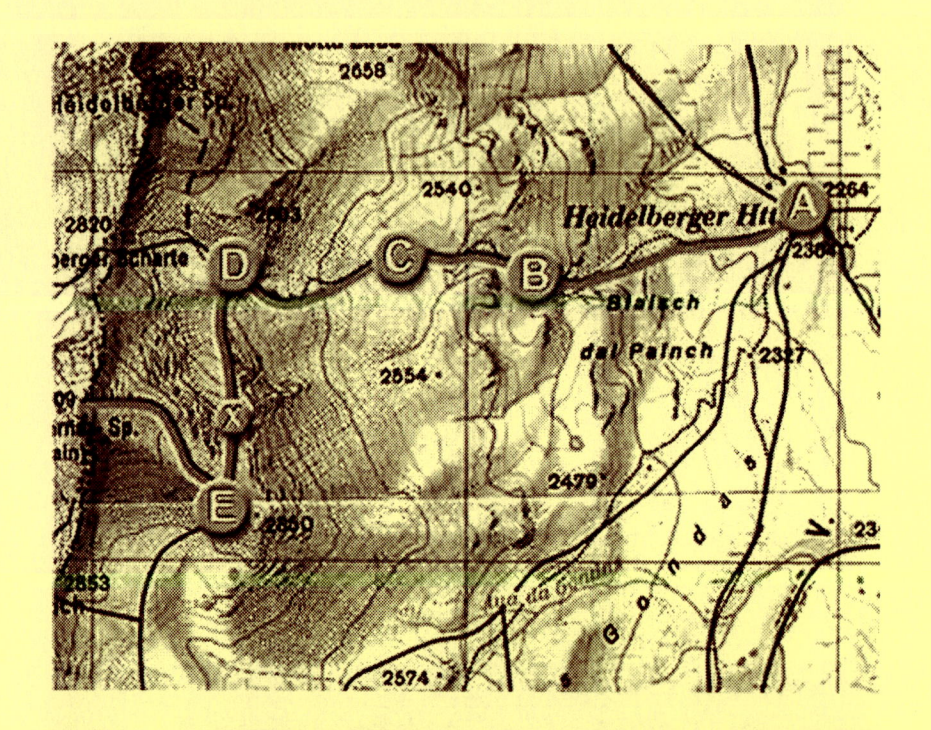

Transferring the information from the map to an image of what is on the ground is an important part of the planning stage.

198 • *A Complete Guide to Ski Touring and Ski Mountaineering*

13 Some Navigation Skills

Navigation for ski touring requires that you are always aware of your position at any given time, that you know the route you have just taken, and that you understand where you are heading. To help you with this you have the practical aids of map, guide book, compass and altimeter, as well as the natural navigation aids of the sun and terrain. The snow often makes it more difficult in as much as some detours may have to be put in to avoid avalanche prone slopes but it also makes some land features unrecognisable. Bad visibility, as in low cloud or snow fall, where white out conditions might prevail, add considerably to the difficulties and increase the danger that you miss your check point by a few metres or possibly walk off the edge of something.

In order to minimise any confusion, your position and that of the features around you should be checked regularly throughout the tour. Even in good weather.

13.1 Understanding the basic winter problems

When touring in winter it is important to be aware of the different conditions. Everything is covered in snow and difficult to recognise. Summer marked paths have disappeared altogether. Navigation and route choice are down to each individual's responsibility. After rising above the protection of the trees you often find yourself in a white landscape, empty of any other colour or contour. When moving uphill you normally have enough time to look around, checking your navigation as you go, but when skiing downhill the speed of forward movement forces you sometimes to make quick decisions on route choice, which might lead to a navigation error. Moving left and right across the slope to find the best snow can often lead to a dead end. Low cloud, blowing snow or wind make visibility poor and sometimes recognising the dangers impossible. When all this makes things too difficult for you, it is time to consider turning round and heading back.

Correct navigation improves safety, not just in bad visibility.

13.2 Maps and Guide Books

Without a map and guide book, planning the tour becomes almost impossible. Between them they allow you to pick out a ski tour to suit your personal ability and then lead you through all the preparations you need to make before setting out.

Legende - Legend - Légende

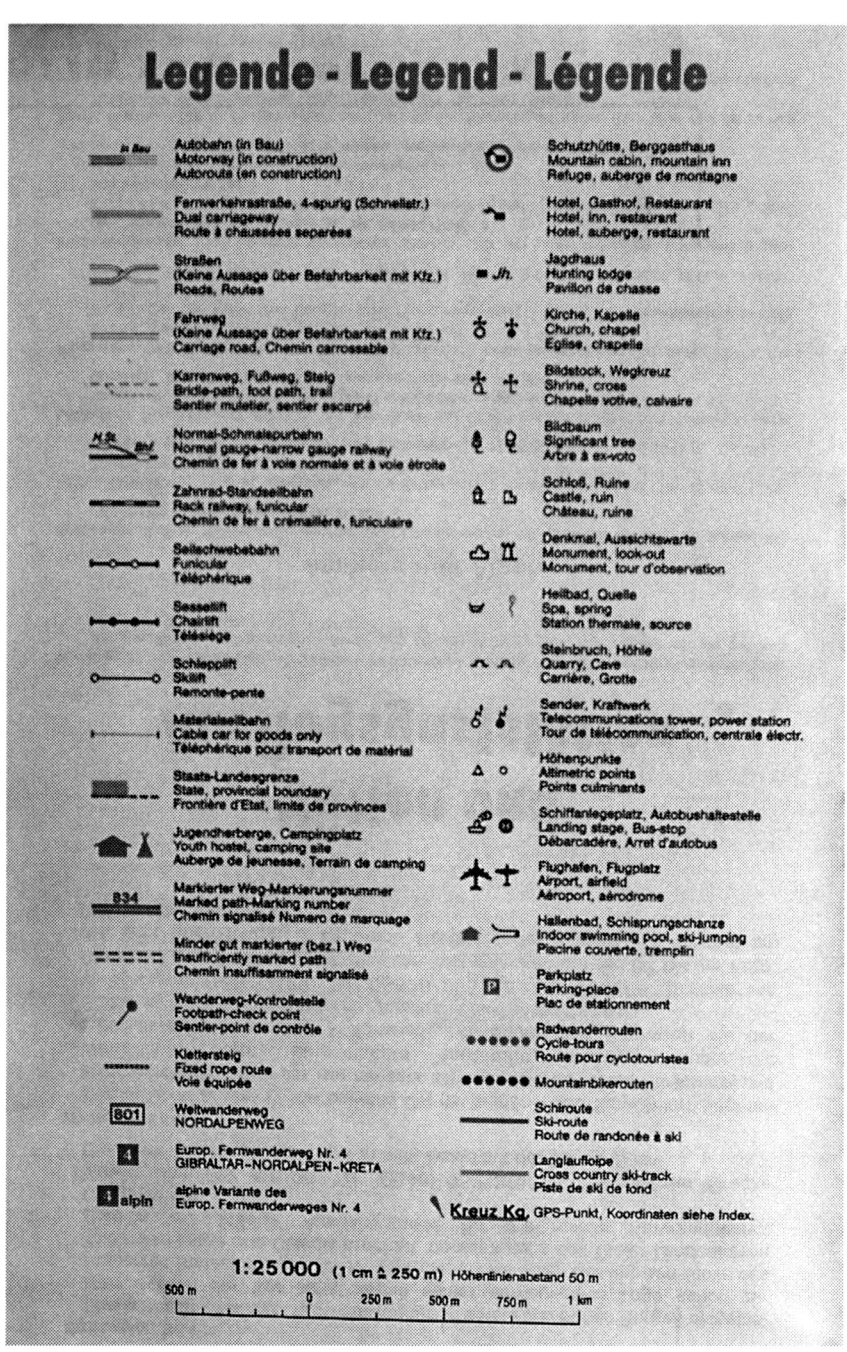

	Autobahn (in Bau)	Motorway (in construction)	Autoroute (en construction)
	Fernverkehrstraße, 4-spurig (Schnellstr.)	Dual carriageway	Route à chaussées separées
	Straßen (Keine Aussage über Befahrbarkeit mit Kfz.)	Roads, Routes	
	Fahrweg (Keine Aussage über Befahrbarkeit mit Kfz.)	Carriage road, Chemin carrossable	
	Karrenweg, Fußweg, Steig	Bridle-path, foot path, trail	Sentier muletier, sentier escarpé
	Normal-Schmalspurbahn	Normal gauge-narrow gauge railway	Chemin de fer à voie normale et à voie étroite
	Zahnrad-Standseilbahn	Rack railway, funicular	Chemin de fer à crémaillère, funiculaire
	Seilschwebebahn	Funicular	Téléphérique
	Sessellift	Chairlift	Télésiège
	Schlepplift	Skilift	Remonte-pente
	Materialseilbahn	Cable car for goods only	Téléphérique pour transport de matériel
	Staats-Landesgrenze	State, provincial boundary	Frontière d'Etat, limite de provinces
	Jugendherberge, Campingplatz	Youth hostel, camping site	Auberge de jeunesse, Terrain de camping
B34	Markierter Weg-Markierungsnummer	Marked path-Marking number	Chemin signalisé Numero de marquage
=====	Minder gut markierter (bez.) Weg	Insufficiently marked path	Chemin insuffisamment signalisé
	Wanderweg-Kontrollstelle	Footpath-check point	Sentier-point de contrôle
	Klettersteig	Fixed rope route	Voie équipée
801	Weitwanderweg NORDALPENWEG		
4	Europ. Fernwanderweg Nr. 4 GIBRALTAR-NORDALPEN-KRETA		
4 alpin	alpine Variante des Europ. Fernwanderweges Nr. 4		
⊖	Schutzhütte, Berggasthaus	Mountain cabin, mountain inn	Refuge, auberge de montagne
	Hotel, Gasthof, Restaurant	Hotel, inn, restaurant	Hotel, auberge, restaurant
Jh.	Jagdhaus	Hunting lodge	Pavillon de chasse
ö †	Kirche, Kapelle	Church, chapel	Eglise, chapelle
	Bildstock, Wegkreuz	Shrine, cross	Chapelle votive, calvaire
	Bildbaum	Significant tree	Arbre à ex-voto
	Schloß, Ruine	Castle, ruin	Château, ruine
	Denkmal, Aussichtswarte	Monument, look-out	Monument, tour d'observation
	Heilbad, Quelle	Spa, spring	Station thermale, source
	Steinbruch, Höhle	Quarry, Cave	Carrière, Grotte
	Sender, Kraftwerk	Telecommunications tower, power station	Tour de télécommunication, centrale électr.
△ ○	Höhenpunkte	Altimetric points	Points culminants
	Schiffanlegeplatz, Autobushaltestelle	Landing stage, Bus-stop	Débarcadère, Arret d'autobus
✈ †	Flughafen, Flugplatz	Airport, airfield	Aéroport, aérodrome
	Hallenbad, Schisprungschanze	Indoor swimming pool, ski-jumping	Piscine couverte, tremplin
P	Parkplatz	Parking-place	Plac de stationnement
••••••	Radwanderrouten	Cycle-tours	Route pour cyclotouristes
••••••	Mountainbikerouten		
	Schiroute	Ski-route	Route de randonée à ski
	Langlaufloipe	Cross country ski-track	Piste de ski de fond
Kreuz Kg.	GPS-Punkt, Koordinaten siehe Index.		

1:25 000 (1 cm ≙ 250 m) Höhenlinienabstand 50 m

500 m 0 250 m 500 m 750 m 1 km

Map legend showing different languages.

13.2.1 Maps

The map is the basic item of navigation for ski touring. The trick is to be able to look at a flat map and visualise it as a relief in 3D. The map is the connection between the actual ground that you will cross and your imagination of what the tour will be like.

Scale

The best scale maps for ski touring are 1:25000. That means that 1cm on the map equals 25000cm or 250m on the ground. 4cm on the map therefore relates to 1km on the ground.

A scale of 1:50000 does not give enough detail for the navigation standard that is often required but is very useful to give an overview of the whole area or in general planning of tours over several days. 1:50000 means that 1cm on the map equals 50000cm or 500m on the ground. 2cm, therefore, is 1km.

To work out the distance on the ground from the map you measure the map in cm or mm and equate it to the following scale:

Working out distance on the ground from the map.					
Distance on the ground	1km	500m	250m	100m	25m
Distance on a 1:25000 map	4cm	2cm	1cm	4mm	1mm
Distance on a 1:50000 map	2cm	1cm	5mm	2mm	0.5mm

Direction

On normal maps North will be at the top and South at the bottom of the map. The text is written from West to East as in a book. Exceptions to this text system are objects that take over a large space and are directional (lakes, glaciers rivers etc) - here the text is written along the object. Alpine maps are now being produced with a grid system as in the UK, for use with GPS. This makes it more accurate for taking bearings from the map and identifying your position.

Map features

Terrain features, as in ridges and saddles, are represented on the map by a series of contour lines. Contour lines join together all areas of the same height. The height difference between each line is the contour interval which varies sometimes from map to map, but for most continental maps it is 20m. This can be checked on the legend at the side of the map. Every fifth contour line is thicker to indicate 100m. You can tell how steep the slope is from the distance the contour lines are apart. Contours close together indicate steep ground; contour lines far apart indicate flat ground. For ski touring it is very important that we learn to recognise the relief from the map as this allows us the safe use of the terrain when setting a track. From the contour lines we can also recognise the aspect of the slope. To do this pick a slope you are considering skiing. Draw a line through the contour line from the top to the bottom that dissects them at 90° and compare this line to the N, S, E and W of your compass.

Maps in Winter

For lots of areas where ski touring is popular there are summer and winter maps. The summer map shows foot paths, the winter maps show ski routes and often avalanche or other danger areas, as well as nature protected areas. To understand what is on the ground the map has a series of symbols - some colour coded to identify things like crevasses, etc. This is important, as in winter, with full snow cover, it is impossible to visually see the crevasses but the map will show you where they are. The type of ground surface is important for avalanches but invisible under a snow blanket. Long grass is a beautiful sliding surface and the map can also give you an indication of this.

Using the Grid

UK ordnance survey maps are all broken down into grid systems. This has the advantage that if you want to let someone know where you are or where you are going you can give them a grid reference. A four figure grid reference gives you a 1km square area, a six figure grid reference gives you a 100m square area and an eight figure grid reference gives you a 10m square area. Each line on the map is numbered and the squares formed by these lines are one kilometre. If the scale of the map is 1:25000 then 4cm on the map is equal to 1km on the ground. When giving a grid reference you always take the number along the bottom first. These are the lines that go from the top of the map to the bottom, north to south and are called the *eastings*. The second half of your grid reference is taken from the numbers on the side of the map - the lines that go across the map from west to east and are called the *northings*. Imagine the square, then, broken down into tenths, or into millimetres. In the two maps below where the first is 1:25000 and the second is 1:50000, the position of the Hoch Vogel summit would have two different grid reference points. The first one is R329 H1434. The second one is 08464845.

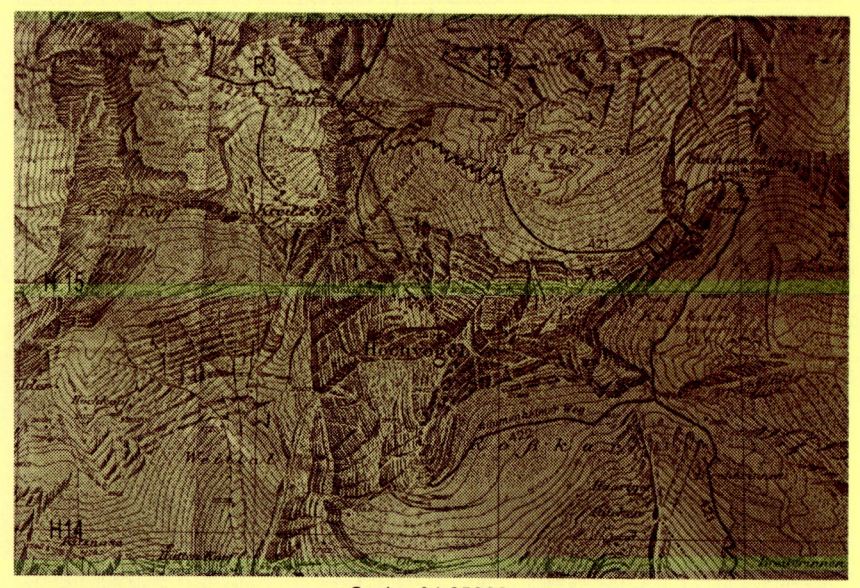

Scale of 1;25000

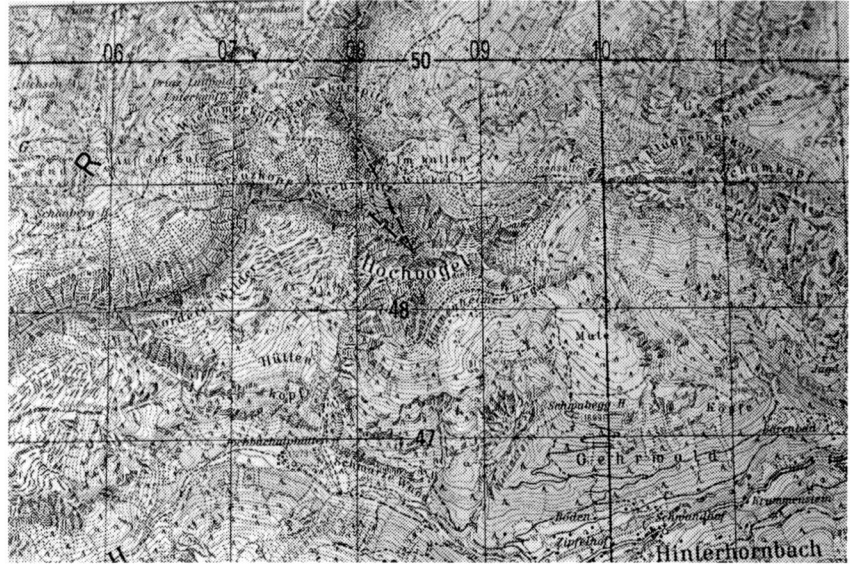

Scale of 1;50000

13.2.2 Guide books

More and more ski touring guide books appear on the market every year, also in English. There are variations to the type of guide book available. A ski touring atlas, for example, will show where ski touring can take place and give examples of a couple of tours for each area. For hut-to-hut touring there is a tendency to show only the main routes connecting the huts with one or two variations. Some only show a selection of the best tours in the area, or from areas lying close to one another. If you intend staying in the same area for more than a few days, it is advisable to get a specific guide book giving all the ski tours for that area.

A detailed ski tour guide book will give you the following information:

- Start point and finish point
- The way up and down
- The time required to ski up and down

- A description of the route
- A map cut-out showing the route
- Quite often a photograph of the route or parts of it
- Any danger areas
- Any avalanche areas
- Where to find up-to-date information on weather and avalanche forecasts
- Alternative options
- Important information, telephone numbers, rescue organisations
- The type of tour
- The equipment needed for the tour
- The difficulty grade of the tour (this grading system often varies from book to book)
- Fitness level required
- Ability required
- Valley accommodation
- Mountain hut details
- A history of the area
- A general knowledge of the area
- Environmental information for the area

With all this information at your fingertips how could you ever think of going ski touring without a guide book? However, a word of warning. A guide book is something written to help you. The author cannot be responsible for you when you are on the tour. Winter conditions can change from day-to-day and the ski tourer must always accept responsibility for his or her own actions and decisions on the ground, especially with a view to route choice, navigation, and evaluation of the alpine dangers and avalanche situation.

13.3 Other aids to navigation

Most people in the UK would never go into the mountains without a compass but when ski touring in the Alps an altimeter is also essential. When searching for the hut in white-out conditions or trying to differentiate between two identical cols, it quickly becomes obvious that a map and guide book is not enough.

Compass

'Always trust your compass', I was told when I was much younger, 'It will give you all the direction information you require'. Most compasses will be broken down into degrees - 360° making up one full circle. East 90°, South 180°, West 270°, and North 360° or 0°. The floating magnetic needle within the housing of the compass (the red end) always points to magnetic north. Magnetic north is different from grid north on the map. This difference is called the magnetic variation. The value of this magnetic variation changes depending on where you are in the world and is always given somewhere on the map. In the Alps it is between 1° - 2°. In the Canadian Rockies it is over 20°. If you were to walk on a compass bearing which had a 4° error for 1km you would be approximately 70m out. You can see therefore that a variation of 1° has little impact, but to forget your variation in Canada could be a disaster for you. The variation is used like so in Europe. If you work out your direction to your next checkpoint on the map, this is called a *grid bearing*. Before you start walking forward on the ground you must now add your variation onto the compass (grid to mag add). If you point the compass at a feature on the ground and want to identify the feature on the map then you are going from a magnetic bearing to a grid bearing and must subtract the variation (mag to grid get rid).

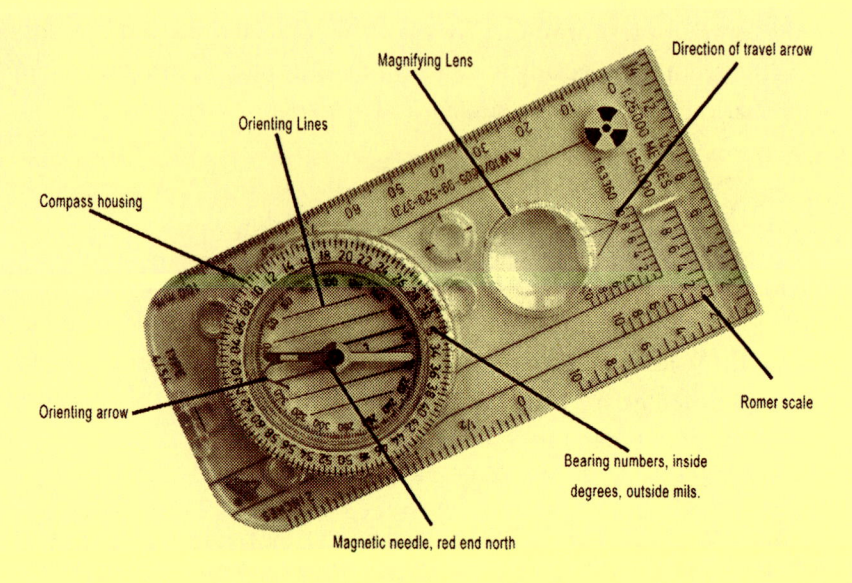

A standard compass for ski touring.

Top tips:

- Always hold the compass flat.

- When using the compass keep it away from metal, electric cables and transceivers, as these all affect the magnetic needle.

- Do not forget the magnetic variation.

- Practice whenever you get the chance.

Altimeter

Because the height is always changing when you are en route on a ski tour (sometimes very quickly on the way down) the altimeter is an invaluable item for pinpointing which contour line you are on. The important thing to be aware of with an altimeter is that it works off barometric pressure. This means, for example, that if you stay overnight in a hut and the weather changes and a low or high pressure approaches, the height of the hut could read differently in the morning. The same thing could happen to you if you are on the move. Therefore, in order to keep the altimeter as accurate as possible, it is important to check it and, if need be, reset it regularly at known heights. Some altimeters come in wristwatch format and can give you a number of useful functions i.e. travelling speed, rate of ascent, total ascent/descent.

An altimeter can be used to assist in making weather predictions as well as showing you what height you are at.

Top tips:

- By noting the exact altitude you can tell how much height difference you have behind you and how much you still have to go.

- If you are moving up or downhill on a compass bearing then the altimeter can tell you at exactly what height you are at - very useful in white-out conditions.

- If you have had to aim for a particular point in bad weather i.e. a hut, and you know the hut lies on a set altitude then the altimeter can be used to contour into it.

A Complete Guide to Ski Touring and Ski Mountaineering

- The altimeter can also be used as a barometer to help with making a weather forecast - very useful if you are on the move for several days. Set the altimeter to the height you are at when overnighting and then check it in the morning. If the height you are at in the morning reads higher then the pressure is dropping and bringing bad weather. If the height in the morning reads lower, then the pressure is rising and bringing good weather.

Binoculars

Very good extras to take on ski tour with you, if you can carry the extra weight, are binoculars. Some are very small and easily packed in a rucksack. The scale should be about 8 x 20 or 8 x 40, which gives you a good compromise between weight, size and function. The 8 means you can see an object 800m away, in the size it would be at 100m to the naked eye.

Uses for binoculars are:

- When you have an overall view of the route ahead, for example in long steady glacier rises, it will allow you to see crevasses from a distance.

- It enables you to observe in detail the route other groups are taking.

- It allows you to get a close-up of the final way up to a summit.

- You are able to plan your route selection from a safe distance i.e. when sitting at the hut, and to compare this to the map.

- You can often recognise snow conditions better i.e. on summit ridges.

Magnifying glass

Some of the detail on maps is quite small or blends in with other detail. When you are in bad light on the ground, in a hut that is badly lit, or if your eyesight is not quite up to it, a magnifying glass comes in very useful. Some compasses come with one built-in or you can buy special ones for the mountains that can also be used to identify snow crystals.

GPS (Global Positioning System)

GPS is a satellite based navigation system made up of a network of satellites orbiting the earth. The GPS enables you to identify your exact position and is accurate to within a few metres, depending on the quality of the device that you have. It works well regardless of weather, visibility, or time of day, but is often unreliable in deep-sided valleys or close to steep rock faces when the signal might not be so clear. Developments over the last few years have improved the function and brought the weight and price down considerably making it a very practical item to carry around with you as a supplement, not an alternative, to a map and compass.

13.4 Using the map and compass

During a ski tour you should always be aware of where you are and where you are going and never simply follow someone else's ski tracks. You should constantly be making observations of terrain features, changes of direction, or timings from one point to another - anything that can be used later on the way back down or if bad weather approaches. The following methods of navigation can be used to keep you on the right track:

Simple aids

The sun can be used to keep you in the correct line of travel. In ski touring season you will find the sun in the east at 0600hrs, in the south at 1200hrs and in the west at 1800hrs. Using a normal watch-face you can identify south by pointing the hour hand at the sun and then bisecting the angle between this and 12 on the watch.

Comparing ground to map

This is the quickest and most common way of checking where you are and what features are around you and visible.

- The first thing to do is to orientate the map to north i.e. make sure the top of the map is facing north. You will now find that any glaciers, rivers, or lifts on the ground run parallel with those seen on the map.

- As well as this you are now trying to relate the contour lines on the map to the features you see in front of you.

- Then, to identify your position, you firstly identify two terrain features that you are facing without moving the map stand on the side of the map so that the features on the map and ground line-up, then draw two imaginary lines back from these features on the map and where the lines cross is your general position.

Orientating the map with the compass

To start making things more accurate it is important to use the compass.

- Turn the housing so that the N lines up with the direction line at the front of the compass.

- Now turn the whole compass until the magnetic needle lays over the top and points in the same direction as the front of the compass.

- Lay the compass on the map and rotate the map separately from the compass until the grid lines that go north to south on the map are parallel with the side of the compass.

Grid bearings

If you know where you are on the map i.e. a hut, and know where you want to go to on the map i.e. a summit, but do not know which direction it is on the ground, you take a grid bearing from the map.

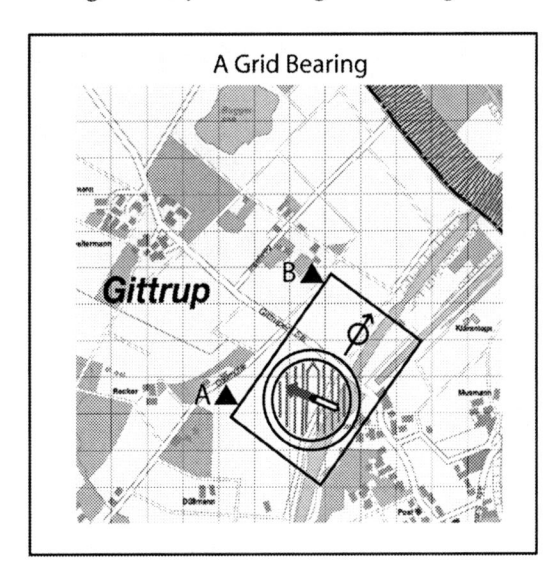

A Grid Bearing

- To do this lay the compass on the map so that the hut and the summit are resting on the side of the compass. Either side will do, but what is very important is that the front of the compass always points towards the feature that you want to go to.

- Keeping the compass fixed on the map you now turn the housing so that the N points to the top of the map and that the lines in the housing are laying parallel with the grid lines on the map that run north to south.

- You now have a grid bearing - you read the bearing from the numbers in the housing which line-up with the front/direction line of the compass.

- If need be, you now add the magnetic variation (grid to mag add).

- Hold the compass flat in your hand in front of your body so that you are looking down at it.

A Complete Guide to Ski Touring and Ski Mountaineering

- Keeping the compass in this position, move yourself round until the magnetic needle and the N mark in the housing line-up with one another. The front of the compass is now pointing in the direction that you should walk, in order to get to your summit.

- Sometimes the feature you are heading for is not visible or the ground in front of you is too steep to take it in a straight line. If this is the case then look ahead for an object on the ground that lies on your compass bearing. When you reach it, check your direction on the compass again. If this is not possible because of bad weather, it might be necessary to send someone in the group out front to the point where you can just see him. Bring him on line with your compass bearing, that person then stands still and the rest of the group zig zag up to him and you repeat the process.

Identifying features ahead of you

Let us say you are skiing along and there is a feature in front of you that you would like to identify. Important to this is that you know your present position.

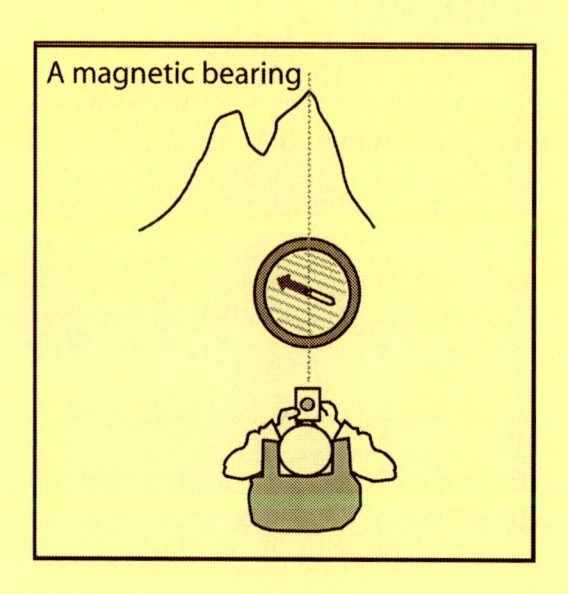

A magnetic bearing

- Hold the compass flat in front of you and point it at the feature you want to identify.

- Turn the housing until the N lines up with the magnetic needle. You now have a magnetic bearing from the point you are standing at to the feature.

- The bearing is read from the number in the housing which is in line with the direction line.

- Estimate what you think the visual distance is from where you are to the feature.

- If need be subtract the magnetic variation (mag to grid get rid).

- Put the compass on the map with the side of the compass on your present position.

- Keeping the side of the compass on your present position, rotate either the map or the compass until the N of the housing is pointing to the top of the map and the lines in the housing are parallel with the grid lines on the map that go north to south.

- Draw a line along the side of the compass towards the front of the compass. Your feature lies somewhere along this line.

- Measure the distance you estimated along the line to make searching for it a little easier.

A resection to find out where you are

If you find yourself in a wide open area and do not know exactly where you are but can recognise the features around you, then doing a resection from two of the features you know can pin point your exact position. Try to pick two features that are far enough apart from one another that the angle they form to you is about 90°.

A resection to identify your position

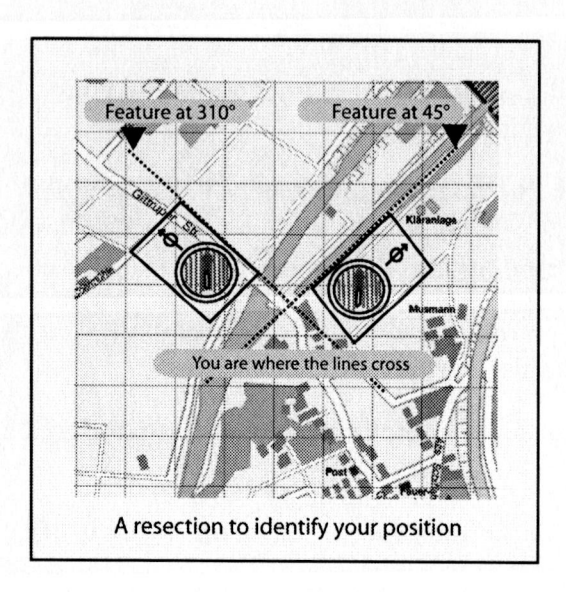

- Take a magnetic bearing to the first of the two features.

- If need be subtract the magnetic variation.

- Place the compass on the map, as before, but this time put the side of the compass on the known feature.

- Keeping the side of the compass on this known feature, line the map and compass up as previously described.

- Draw a line along the side of the compass, this time going from the known feature to the back of the compass.

- Repeat the process with the second feature.

- Where the two lines cross on the map is your position.

- If you are using an altimeter and know at which height you are i.e. on which contour line you are standing, all you need is one feature. Using the process described above to draw a line on the map, your position is where the line crosses your contour line. The more the contour line and the feature at right angle to one another are, the more accurate your position will be.

13.5 Measuring distance

Sometimes it is important to know precisely how far you have travelled. Mostly it is in times of bad visibility when you have to be certain of the distance to avoid some danger, or to turn left or right at the correct time. The compass gives you the direction but it does not identify for you how far you have travelled along this direction. In most cases when it is white-out conditions you will be moving very slowly. Here are a few ideas to help you measure distance:

GPS

A good GPS, when used correctly, can tell you exactly to the metre how far you have travelled since your last stop. Plus, it will give you the speed you are moving at.

Altimeter

When you are skiing up or down in bad visibility the altimeter will give you the distance you have travelled from your last stop, in as much as it can tell you the height that you have gained or lost since your last stop - the altitude you are at compared with the altitude that you were at. You then have to measure the distance between these two points on the map.

Timing

On a flat or slightly undulating ground the pace tends to be fairly constant. An average speed when skiing with skins on is about 3km per hour. This obviously varies in heavy snow. A worthwhile exercise is to measure an exact distance of 100m or 200m and mark it at both ends. Then time yourself up and down between the points, sometimes in the fresh snow, sometimes in a good track, and you will eventually build up your average speed in all types of snow conditions.

Pacing

Believe it or not you can pace on skis exactly as you would do in summer. Obviously not when skiing downhill, but when you are moving with skins on. Measure an exact distance as in the timing exercises above, but then try pacing i.e. counting every second step, and see how this compares to your summer values.

Measuring ski lengths

This method works out fairly accurately and, after a bit of practice, you can move quite quickly. Your ski length will probably be about 170cm or maybe 180cm. Stand still and mark the snow at the tail of your ski and then put a second mark in front of your ski (the estimated amount to bring it up to 2m). Then walk forward until the tail of the ski is at the second mark and repeat this 50 times, you have now gone 100m. This would be something you could do for a few hundred metres to get out of difficulty. You could also measure 1m on your ski, mark it with a pen or tape and measure 100m as above.

Using a rope

If you have in your rucksack a length of rope (say 10m x 3mm - something which takes up very little space), hold one end of the rope in your hand and have someone else in the group hold the other end (both right hand or left hand but not alternate), so that he is behind you and the rope is taut. You are now 10 metres apart. Make a mark in the snow. Keeping the rope taut move forward until the rear person reaches the mark and repeat the process 10 times for 100m. With practice, this can be done without stopping.

On a glacier

On a glacier you would be roped-up in bad visibility. A 3-man team 8m apart would put the front person 16m away from the back person. Working on the system above, the front person makes a mark in the snow. The team move forward until the back person is at the mark and communicates to the front person to make another mark. The process is repeated enough times to make up the distance you require. 6 times would be 96m.

Although you are unlikely to ever use some of these methods on a nice sunny day, it is worth practicing them in good weather before you need them for real, when the wrong step forward might be the one that goes over the edge.

14 Protecting the Environment

Ski touring in a winter wonderland, the quietness of rhythmically skinning up the side of a mountain, beautiful views of an untouched landscape, time to yourself, time to meditate as you sit there on your own on a summit staring out on a wilderness, enjoying your hard earned packed lunch, breathing fresh, crisp mountain air: a definite remedy from the stress of city life that I am sure any doctor would recommend.

Unfortunately, as more and more people realise the benefits of ski touring the chances of sitting on a summit on your own are less and less likely. Increased skiing ability through improved equipment, ever increasing lift prices, overcrowded pistes, long lift queues, and boring piste runs, all drive skiers away from the pistes and towards ski touring. Experts estimate that there is approximately 15 times more ski touring happening now than there was a few years ago. What at one time was the domain of environmentally-conscious, enthusiastic mountain people is now becoming the location for the overspill of good, bad and indifferent piste skiers - some with limited knowledge of nature and its many users.

With so many people now using the mountains in winter it is important that we understand what the mountains do for us and other users, and what we as ski tourers can do to protect the landscape we enjoy so much, and to preserve it as it is for future generations, without taking away our own right to use and enjoy it.

What is it that we are trying to look after?

- The Alps are the habitat for many types of animals, birds and plants.
- Glaciers, streams and snow, which eventually melts into the rivers, offer many towns and cities in Europe a high standard of drinking water.
- Clean air masses move in and over the Alps

Getting to the start

Most ski tourers travel by car, although some ski tours lend themselves very well to travel with public transport, on a cable car or similar lift system. Most people are well aware of the damage caused by car exhaust fumes and this is even more so in deep-sided valleys where the air does not circulate so easily. Another problem with cars is that a lot of tours start in the middle of nowhere with narrow roads and very limited parking and it happens sometimes that tourers block roads with inconsiderate parking. This obviously makes life difficult for snow ploughs trying to clear the road, essential services, or even the locals going about their daily routine. The solutions are also very well known: if possible use public transport, team up with others to cut down on the amount of cars used, or get someone to drop you off and to pick you up at the end, obeying any traffic signs no matter how far away you are from a main road.

On tour

The Alps, with its woodland, offers its inhabitants much in the way of protection. There is a natural protection against avalanches. In times of heavy rain it soaks up water and in dry periods gives it slowly back. This all helps avoid erosion and adds to the good supply of drinking water. It offers an income for foresters and offers protection and food supply for many animals. When ski touring, we tend to leave the normal summer paths behind. Much damage can be done with sharp ski edges in times of thin snow cover, or animals are startled in heavy snow cover as we venture from these paths. Winter has less in the way of food for animals than the summer and a startled animal running uphill in heavy snow has a much higher energy output (if you do not believe me then try it yourself) which needs to be replaced with a food intake that is quite simply not there. For these reasons it is important that we think about our actions and try to show some consideration for our surroundings.

Bushes and shrubs are home to a variety of wild life. Choose your line well so as not to disturb them.

What we can do

- Obey signs and local rules. In some countries you are not allowed to enter young woodland with trees under 3m in height. Austria has put a ban on skiing woodland on both sides of the piste for a distance of 500m, and the same both sides of lifts except in specific areas given to ski touring. Fines for breaking the rules are hefty and an excuse of not understanding the signs is not accepted.

- Keep an eye out for animals and give them time to move away slowly...stop and watch them and you may also learn something of their habits.

- On Swiss maps the protected areas are marked. Stay out of them.

- Try to set an example by avoiding what you think are, or should be, protected areas and your actions will hopefully educate some of the not so knowledgeable tourers around you.

- Be prepared to compromise a little. It is nice in Spring, when there is not so much snow left, to try and keep the skis on, hopping from snow patch to snow patch all the way to the bottom. Think of the damage you may be causing to grass and young plants beginning to grow and think about taking your skis off earlier.

- Light forest and bush areas are home to a variety of bird life, mainly on south facing slopes and up to about 1600m. Birds like Grouse and Ptarmigan are not capable of storing fat the way hibernating animals (Marmot) do and must therefore eat daily from their hoarded supplies or from what they find out and about. They are creatures of habit and have a daily routine which does not change much. To conserve energy they often sleep up for as many as 20 hours a day and are only actively in search of food for a couple of hours 0700 - 1000hrs and 1600 - 1700hrs. They tend to fly constantly in a gliding flight downhill and walk back uphill, eating as they go. To startle them during these times means that they do not eat that day. To startle them a few days in a row is life-threatening for them. Get used to avoiding their living space.

- Some guide books give good information about local wildlife habits. Take time to read them.

- Finally. If we all took our rubbish back down the hill with us it would certainly go a long way to help. If you had enough energy to carry bags full of food up with you then you must certainly have enough energy and space in your rucksack to carry empty bags and rubbish back down again.

Take time out to observe the environment and you might learn more about your surroundings.

15 Some Useful Addresses and Literature

Austrian Alpine Club (UK)
12A North Street
Wareham
Dorset
BH20 4AG
Tel: 0870 242 7309
Website: http://www.aacuk.org.uk
E-mail: manager@aacuk.org.uk

British Association of Snowsport Instructors
Glenmore
Aviemore
Inverness-shire, PH22 1QU
Tel: 01479 861717
Fax: 01479 861718
Website: www.basi.org.uk
E-mail: basi@basi.org.uk

Glenmore Lodge
Aviemore
Inverness-shire, PH22 1QU
Tel: 01479 861256
E-mail: enquiries@glenmorelodge.org.uk

British Mountaineering Council
177-179 Burton Road
Manchester
M20 2BB
Tel: 0161 445 4747
Fax: 0161 445 4500
Website: www.thebmc.co.uk

St John's Ambulance
St Andrews Ambulance Association
British Red Cross
(All of these should be listed in your local telephone directory)

British Association of Ski Patrollers
20 Lorne Drive
Glencoe
Argyll, PH49 4HR
Tel; 01855 811 443
Fax: 01855 811 678
Website: www.basp.org.uk
E-mail: firstaid@basp.org.uk

The mountain skills training handbook	Hill and Johnston	ISBN 0-71531091-7
Rock climbing essential skill and techniques	Peters	ISBN 0-9541511-1-9
Hill walking MLT handbook Vol 1		ISBN 0-9541511-0-0
Avalanche safety for skiers and climbers	Tony Daffern	ISBN 0-906371-26-0
BASI Alpine manual		ISBN 0-904212-06-8

16 Alpine Huts

A brief history

Around 1860, Alpine clubs started appearing all over Europe. Although not alpine in nature, Britain was first to form an Alpine club, closely followed by other European countries. The general idea was to try to bring like-minded people together, to foster a love for the Alps and at the same time bring income to the poor farming areas of the Alps where the richer people, from the industrial areas, were starting to take their holidays. Accommodation in this new playground was required and the clubs started to build huts in their favourite areas. Each country's club was split into sections and sponsors were sought to finance the building of these huts with some of the huts being named after the section which built it. Britain's modern equivalent of what the alpine countries would understand as the alpine club is the British Mountaineering Council, although there is also a UK Section of the Austrian Alpine Club (AAC) which has almost 5000 members. The Austrian Alpine Club itself boasts over 300,000 members.

Communication between the clubs must have been quite good because the huts that sprang up were well-placed to link-up the more popular tours over several days. Most of the huts are between 4 and 8 hours walk apart. Communication between the clubs remains good and members from one club enjoy reciprocal rights in huts owned by other clubs.

Each section is responsible for maintaining the huts they own and for the paths in and out of their area. Those sections with no direct ownership contribute to a fund for the general upkeep of the huts and environment. Much of the work done is carried out by volunteers from the various sections, although technical know-how and equipment is very expensive.

A welcome sight at the end of the day.

Membership benefits

- Members are given priority over non-members on sleeping space.

- Members get substantially reduced rates in the huts (6 - 8 nights in a hut will more or less justify the cost of membership).

- Mountain rescue is covered (certainly with the AAC) as part of the membership fee.

- Newsletters and club meets are part of the norm.

- Members can bring their own food to eat in the hut.

Hut rules

For the comfort of everyone staying at the huts, the Alpine clubs have a set of rules that are much the same in every country. Some of the more important ones are:

- Quiet hour is 2200hrs.

- No boots past the common room area (some are no boots inside the hut).

- No smoking past the common room area (some are totally non-smoking).

- No ice axe, crampons etc to be carried into the sleeping areas.

- Everyone should have their own hut sleeping bag (not really a sleeping bag, more a light weight sleeping bag liner). This is to keep the blankets cleaner.

An alpine hut at its best during the ski touring season.

Hut etiquette

- It is customary for the leader of the group to make contact with the hut guardian, find out where everything is and then go back and pass this on to the group. This avoids the guardian getting stressed out by everyone individually asking the same questions.

- Groups should book the hut in advance, to allow the hut staff to plan ahead for food and sleeping space.

- Some huts have different systems on how the beds are allocated. Some wait until they think most people will have arrived before allocating beds. Some take priority from the hut book - so if your name is not in you will be last to get a bed. Some allocate as you come in. It is worth while checking this as soon as you arrive.

- The leader should ensure that the group knows the hut rules and what they mean i.e. sleeping areas are for sleeping and not for conversation.

- Think about the fact that you might be making an early start. Organise your kit accordingly so that you are not packing for an hour in the morning. There is nothing worse than the constant rustle of plastic bags and loud whispers at 0400hrs. You should be able to pick up your gear silently and move downstairs within about five minutes.

- 2200hrs is quiet hour, not last orders. Most continentals in the huts will have a few drinks in the afternoon or early evening but stop early enough to let it run through. In a dormitory sleeping twenty or more people it is not a good idea to have to get up for the toilet or to have a steady flow of people getting up every fifteen minutes throughout the night. In some of the huts you might well be hoping that you do not have to make that move.

- Members are allowed to eat their own food in the hut but the guardian makes money out of people buying his food. He may ask you to vacate your table until the paying customers have been fed. This is normal.

- Make sure you fill in the hut book.

- Take your rubbish with you.

Time to relax after a hard day.

Type of huts

The huts vary in style, standard and quality quite considerably. This could be for any number of reasons - their remoteness, the wealth of the section, their willingness to invest in the hut, the popularity of the hut in the amount of visitors, or even the hut staff.

Some huts are mountain hotels offering sleeping space to over two hundred people and a menu second to none. Some are just a shed offering shelter. Some offer beds in smaller rooms as well as dormitories. Some have hot showers, and some have no running water.

Not all huts are suitable for ski touring, much depends on their location. A good indication will be the times of year that the hut is open. Most of the huts are open from June to September, but this varies a little depending on their altitude and remoteness. If the hut is open for ski touring it may be open from Christmas to Easter, if it is easily accessible, but the huts in the higher areas for ski touring will more than likely be open from mid March until beginning of May.

Thank you

We are grateful to a number of people in the production of this book.

Caroline Jenns, Andy and Jenny Luxon for proof reading.

Tim Walker for the foreword and advice.

Thanks to Dave Whiteman for the technical photos and for his patience during the endless retakes high up on the glacier in Pitztal.

Allgau PC for the illustrations.

Friends too many to mention who helped with the photos.

Thanks to our sponsors for providing clothing and technical gear and for their support of the book. Haglofs, DMM and Mamut, Petzl, British Association of Snowsport Instructors (BASI), Glenmore Lodge, Pitztal Tourist office, Nevisport, Point Venture, Nordicblowfish,

THE ABC OF LIFE SAVING:

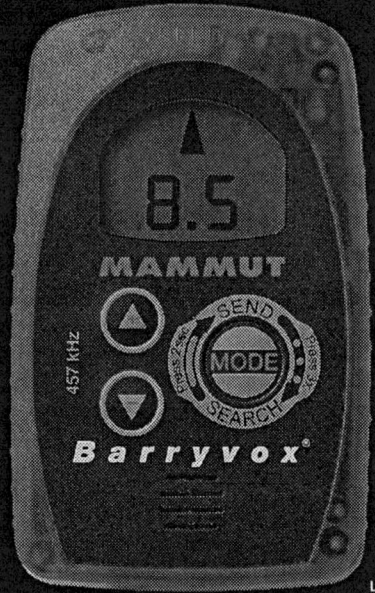

Absolute Swiss Quality

457 kHz

Barryvox®

Life size

A: SWITCH ON SEARCH MODE
B: FOLLOW DISPLAY INSTRUCTIONS
C: RESCUE

MAMMUT

Locating people buried under avalanches is faster and more reliable with MAMMUT Barryvox. The basic functions have been optimized for simple operation. Technical data: small and light (170 g including batteries), approx. 60 m range, can transmit for over 300 hours. Additional functions for professionals. For further informations please visit our Web site our contact DMM International Ltd., Phone +44 (0) 1286 873 595, info@dmmwales.com, www.mammut.ch

HAGLÖFS

Outstanding Outdoor Equipment

HAGLÖFS DEUTSCHLAND GMBH
Albert-Einstein-Str. 6
87437 Kempten
www.haglofs.se
info@haglofs.de

glenmorelodge
a sportscotland national centre

need an adventure?

LEARN / DEVELOP / QUALIFY

SKI MOUNTAINEERING & TOURING IN SCOTLAND & THE ALPS

call or go on-line to find out more!

www.glenmorelodge.org.uk

Tel: 01479 861256

inspiring adventure

pointventure

- Guided Tours
- Avalanche Awareness
- Hut to Hut

▲ Introductory Courses
▲ Ski Touring
▲ Ski Mountaineering
▲ Off-Piste Skiing

Contact:
Sam Burns
Email: samburns@pointventure.de
Information: www.pointventure.de
Mobil: 01752069481

professional
TRAINING AND QUALIFICATIONS

> Qualifications valid and well-respected throughout the world

> GAP year programmes and fast track retrenchment opportunities

> For top-quality instruction in all Snowsports Disciplines - look for a BASI Instructor!

For more info:
British Association of Snowsport Instructors

Glenmore · Aviemore
Inverness-shire PH22 1QU · Scotland

Tel +44 (0)1479 861717
Fax +44 (0)1479 861718
Email basi@basi.org.uk

www.basi.org.uk

www.pitztal.com
...der Urlaub kann beginnen!

- 80 Pistenkilometer
- Pitztaler Gletscher bis 3440m und Rifflsee
- Familienskigebiet Hochzeiger
- Bambinifreipass für Kinder unter 10 Jahren
- Apres´ski und Hüttengaudi
- Loipen und geräumte Winterwanderwege
- Rodelabende und Eisklettern

- 400km Wanderwege
- zahlreiche Hütten und Almen
- 42 km Mountainbikestrecke
- Pitzis Kinderclub
- kostenloser talweiter Bade- und Wanderbus
- Pitztaler Almenweg
- attraktive Veranstaltungen

PITZTAL

TOURISMUSVERBAND PITZTAL · A-6473 Wenns/Pitztal
Tel. +43(0)5414/86999 · Fax. +43(0)5414/86999-88
e-mail: info@pitztal.com · www.pitztal.com

Love climbing? Hate shopping?
www.nevisport.com

nevisport

nordicblowfish

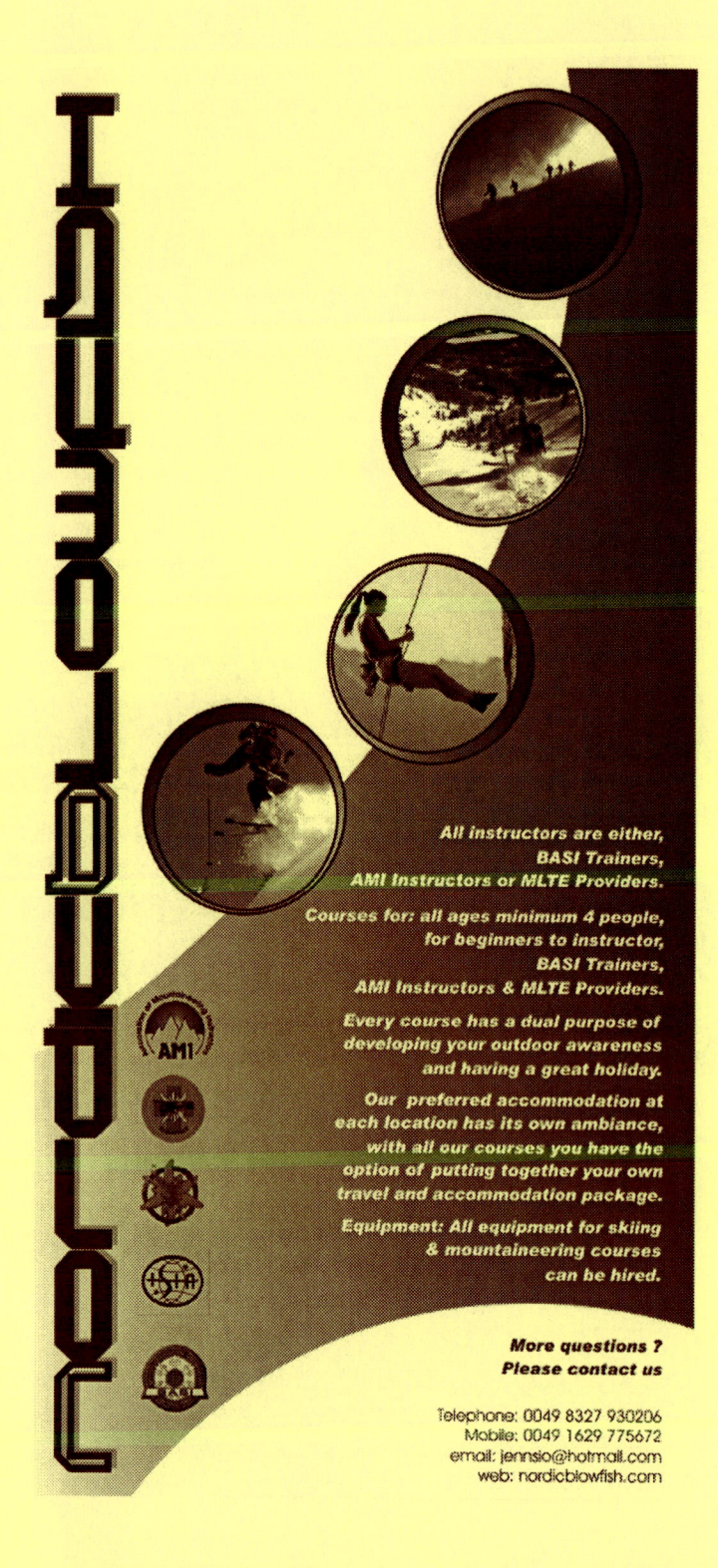

All instructors are either,
BASI Trainers,
AMI Instructors or MLTE Providers.

Courses for: all ages minimum 4 people,
for beginners to instructor,
BASI Trainers,
AMI Instructors & MLTE Providers.

Every course has a dual purpose of
developing your outdoor awareness
and having a great holiday.

Our preferred accommodation at
each location has its own ambiance,
with all our courses you have the
option of putting together your own
travel and accommodation package.

Equipment: All equipment for skiing
& mountaineering courses
can be hired.

**More questions ?
Please contact us**

Telephone: 0049 8327 930206
Mobile: 0049 1629 775672
email: jennsio@hotmail.com
web: nordicblowfish.com

Slide or Glide

Why not try Hindelang for your next or even first ski touring expedition ideally situated on the borders of Austria, Switzerland and Germany **Slide or Glide** can offer the ideal base for all grades of ski tour from novice to expert. Access from UK could not be easier, we are 90 Mins by road or rail from the three international airports of Friedrichshafen, Munich and Stuttgart. Transfers can be arranged. There are over a dozen tours within 5km of the front door.

Slide or Glide

Accommodation/Bar/Bistro with the mountain hut atmosphere
20 Minutes from high Alpine tours up to 2400m
Safety equipment, training & local knowledge available
www.slideorglide.net
Info@slideorglide.net
0049(0)8324 973670

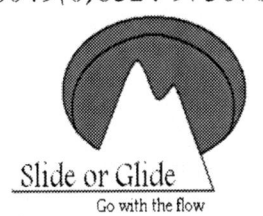

Slide or Glide
Go with the flow

Lightning Source UK Ltd.
Milton Keynes UK
25 October 2010

161881UK00001B/70/A